WALKI

NORTH Y

WESTERN

Paul Hannon

HILLSIDE

HILLSIDE GUIDES - ACROSS THE NORTH

Long Distance Walks

- THE COAST TO COAST WALK
- DALES WAY COMPANION
- THE WESTMORLAND WAY
- NORTH BOWLAND TRAVERSE
- FURNESS WAY
- CLEVELAND WAY COMPANION
- THE CUMBERLAND WAY
- LADY ANNE'S WAY

Circular Walks - Lancashire

- BOWLAND
- PENDLE & THE RIBBLE

Circular Walks - Yorkshire Dales

- HOWGILL FELLS
- THREE PEAKS
- MALHAMDALE
- WHARFEDALE
- NIDDERDALE
- WENSLEYDALE
- SWALEDALE

Circular Walks - North York Moors

- BOOK ONE - WESTERN MOORS
- BOOK TWO - SOUTHERN MOORS
- BOOK THREE - NORTHERN MOORS

Circular Walks - South Pennines

- BRONTE COUNTRY
- CALDERDALE
- ILKLEY MOOR

Circular Walks - North Pennines

- TEESDALE
- EDEN VALLEY

Hillwalking - Lake District

- OVER LAKELAND MOUNTAINS
- OVER LAKELAND FELLS

Yorkshire Pub Walks

- HARROGATE/WHARFE VALLEY
- HAWORTH/AIRE VALLEY

Large format colour hardback

FREEDOM OF THE DALES

BIKING COUNTRY
- YORKSHIRE DALES CYCLE WAY
- WEST YORKSHIRE CYCLE WAY
- MOUNTAIN BIKING - WEST/SOUTH YORKSHIRE

- WALKING COUNTRY TRIVIA QUIZ

Over 1000 questions on the great outdoors

WALKING COUNTRY

NORTH YORK MOORS
WESTERN

Paul Hannon

HILLSIDE

HILLSIDE
PUBLICATIONS
11 Nessfield Grove
Keighley
West Yorkshire
BD22 6NU

First published in 1988 in different format
This fully revised and extended 4th edition
first published 1996

ISBN 1 870141 34 2

For Rebecca

Whilst the author has walked and researched all the routes for the purposes of this guide, no responsibility can be accepted for any unforeseen circumstances encountered while following them. The publisher would, however, greatly appreciate any information regarding material changes, and any problems encountered.

Cover illustration: Cold Moor from Cringle Moor
Back cover: Whitestone Cliff;   Rievaulx Abbey;
Winter on Hasty Bank;   Springtime at Ampleforth
(Paul Hannon/Big Country Picture Library)

Page 1: old guidestone under Cringle Moor
Page 3: Rievaulx Bridge

Printed in Great Britain by
Carnmor Print & Design
95-97 London Road
Preston
Lancashire
PR1 4BA

CONTENTS

INTRODUCTION

THE NORTH YORK MOORS NATIONAL PARK

The North York Moors is the fourth largest of our National Parks, designated in 1952 with an area of 553 square miles. It is probably the best-defined upland area of all, rising island-like from the surrounding countryside. This creates an impression of much greater altitude than its very modest summit of 1490 feet attains. If asked which of the parks is bottom of the height table, few would be likely to provide the correct answer, the North York Moors.

To the north is the Cleveland Plain, westwards the Vales of Mowbray and York, and southwards the Vale of Pickering, while to the east is the ultimate low point, the North Sea. The park itself however has a solid upland mass spreading from the centre towards the western escarpments, where one can walk for mile upon mile and lose little altitude. It is, of course, all this heather-clad moorland for which the North York Moors National Park is best known.

Heather moors, despite their profusion, are only one aspect of this diverse region, for here are some delightful green valleys and a spectacular length of coastline composed largely of rugged cliffs. There are sandy shorelines and rocky coves, and inland some shapely summits, fascinating rock outcrops, and beautiful waterfalls: and, despite all the forestry, some enchanting indigenous woods. The hand of man appears to have been laid everywhere, even on the lonely moortops littered with ancient burial mounds and standing stones. The scores of villages range from fishing ports to moorland farming communities, though many of the villages are to be found beneath the hills, taking advantage of the shelter.

Man has also left ruined abbeys and castles; old roads including famous drovers' routes and Roman roads, and countless paved trods and packways going back to medieval times; absorbing relics of the former ironstone, alum and jet industries; and not least of all an unrivalled collection of wayside crosses, some being ancient christian symbols, and others serving as waymarks or boundary stones.

This is walkers' territory par excellence, with a plethora of long distance and challenge walks crossing it. Best known are the first, the Lyke Wake Walk, and the longest and best, the Cleveland Way, while the Coast to Coast Walk concludes here.

The Western Moors

The subject of this volume is the western area of the Park, dominated by the ranges of the Cleveland Hills and the Hambleton Hills, but including their lovely hinterland descending into upper Ryedale and Bilsdale.

Together these hills extend from the White Horse of Kilburn to Roseberry Topping above Great Ayton, and they form the western boundary of the Moors throughout their entire length. The very northern limits, around Roseberry Topping, will feature in a new edition of the companion volume *North York Moors - Northern*. It is midway, above Osmotherley, that the Cleveland and Hambleton Hills merge, and the contrast in their respective characters can easily be discerned.

On Sutton Bank, looking to Roulston Scar and Hood Hill

Running south, the Hambletons take the form of a broad and undulating whaleback ridge, and for the most part support good agricultural land almost to the top: the steep outer scarp holds much woodland. To the north meanwhile, the Cleveland Hills are far more aggressive animals rising to some shapely and individual tops, with high heather moors reaching into the heart of the park: these hills extend in dog-leg fashion above the Cleveland Plain, and besides being blighted by forestry on their lower outer slopes, they bear the scars of a once thriving quarrying industry.

Rising in the shadow of the two hill ranges, the river Rye flows through delectable sylvan environs to create a perfect foil to the open moors above. The nature of the terrain dictates that most villages stand on the easy ground at the very foot of the scarps, but 'inside' the moors Chop Gate, Hawnby and Old Byland certainly imbibe the invigorating moorland air.

Getting around

The area is bounded by the A19/A172 Stokesley-Thirsk road to the west, while the A170 Thirsk-Helmsley road and the B1257 Helmsley-Stokesley road best serve the area, running through it as they do. Public transport on the former is good, though services quickly deteriorate on the other two. Many of the villages are at best infrequently served, some not at all. The nearest railway stations are at Thirsk to the west and the tiny ones on the Esk Valley line leaving Middlesbrough to the north. With a little planning, a number of permutations can be created by linking different sections of the walks, either to create longer routes or to take advantage of public transport.

Using the guide

Each walk is self-contained, with essential information being followed by a simple map and concise description of the route. Dovetailed between this are useful notes of features along the way, and interspersed are illustrations which both capture the flavour of the walks and document the many items of interest. Please remember to obey legitimate signs encountered on your walks: rights of way can be opened, closed or diverted. On these occasions the official notices should take precedence over the guidebook.

The simple sketch maps identify the location of the routes rather than the fine detail, and whilst the route description should be sufficient to guide you around, an Ordnance Survey map is recommended. The route as depicted can easily be plotted on the relevant OS map. To gain the most from a walk, the remarkable detail of the Outdoor Leisure maps cannot be matched: they also serve to vary walks as desired, giving an improved picture of one's surroundings and the availability of linking paths. This area is particularly fortunate in that just one sheet gives comprehensive coverage of the walks:

Sheet 26 - North York Moors, Western area

Also extremely useful for general planning purposes are the Landranger sheets, at 1:50,000. The following cover the area:

93 - Middlesbrough & Darlington; 94 - Whitby;
99 - Northallerton & Ripon; 100 - Malton & Pickering

In addition, North York Moors 1-inch Tourist Map covers the whole area.

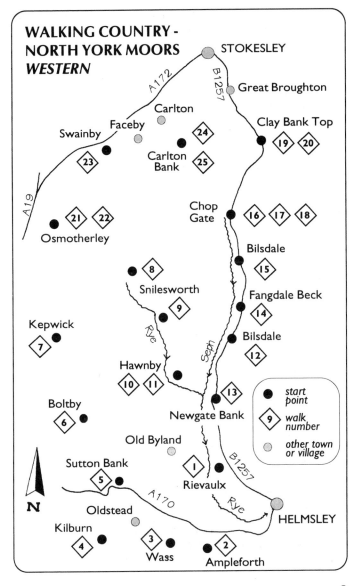

WALKING COUNTRY -
NORTH YORK MOORS
WESTERN

STOKESLEY

Great Broughton

A172

B1257

Carlton

Faceby

Swainby

⟨24⟩

Clay Bank Top

⟨19⟩ ⟨20⟩

⟨23⟩

Carlton
Bank

⟨25⟩

A19

Chop
Gate

⟨16⟩ ⟨17⟩ ⟨18⟩

⟨21⟩ ⟨22⟩

Osmotherley

Bilsdale

⟨15⟩

⟨8⟩

Snilesworth

Fangdale Beck

⟨9⟩

⟨14⟩

Rye

Bilsdale

Kepwick

⟨12⟩

⟨7⟩

Seph

Hawnby

⟨10⟩ ⟨11⟩

⟨13⟩

Boltby

Newgate Bank

⟨6⟩

Old Byland

	start point
●	
⟨9⟩	walk number
●	other town or village

Sutton Bank

⟨1⟩

⟨5⟩

Rievaulx

B1257

Oldstead

A170

Rye

Kilburn

HELMSLEY

⟨4⟩

⟨3⟩

⟨2⟩

N

Wass

Ampleforth

9

RIEVAULX ABBEY

START *Rievaulx*   *Grid ref. SE 575849*

DISTANCE *6½ miles*

ORDNANCE SURVEY MAPS
1:50,000
Landranger 100 - Malton & Pickering
1:25,000
Outdoor Leisure 26 - North York Moors West

ACCESS *Start from the village centre. The abbey has a good car park for visitors to the ruins. Numerous spaces are available on the adjacent roadside. Seasonal bus service from Helmsley. Alternative starts are Old Byland, mid-walk, or the entrance to Nettledale.*

Generally easy walking above and below the wooded slopes of Ryedale. Not forgetting the famous ruin.

S Rievaulx Abbey dates from the 12th century and vies with that other great house of the Cistercians, Fountains, in the beauty of its wooded environs. There is however a very imposing grandeur here that is virtually unparalleled: perhaps not surprisingly, the abbey took over a century to build. It is now in the care of English Heritage. High on the hillside above (reached by continuing up the lane through the hamlet - note the thatched cottages) are the delightfully laid out Rievaulx Terraces complete with two temples. Created by the Duncombe family in the 18th century, the National Trust now maintains the site.

From the abbey take the road north into the hamlet, and after a handful of buildings take a gate on the left ('footpath to Bow Bridge'). Cross a stable yard and a paddock before continuing away alongside a hedge. Just over it are the scant remains of a canal that brought locally quarried stone to the abbey construction site. **The straight line eventually takes us to the bank of the river Rye. A sketchy path heads upstream, but with Bow Bridge ahead, leave the river for a stile onto an enclosed track which drops down to the shapely bridge. Shortly after it take a stile on the right and head away alongside a fence. At the end the river is rejoined, and traced on boardwalks through a steep wooded bank. Emerging, forsake the river again and cross straight over the pasture to a stile onto a farm road.**

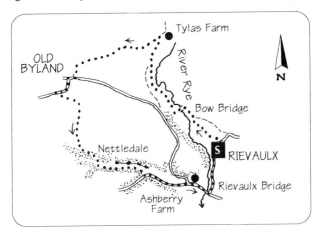

Follow this farm road right to its demise above Tylas Farm. The name is a corruption of its original name, Tile House: this was to have been the location of 'Byland' Abbey - see note below on Old Byland. **Here turn up the rough track to the left for a steep climb to Tylas Barn.** This opens up glorious views over wooded Ryedale, with the abbey just visible down-dale. **Beyond the barn the track runs easier to the well defined head of tiny Oxendale. From a stile just in front an invisible field path heads directly away, keeping to the edge of four fields.** We have vast wide open landscapes, though little evidence of the moors other than Roppa's moor to the north-east. **At the end of the fourth - with no further stiles - turn left to run in another straight line to a stile onto a back road. Turn right and then left to enter Old Byland.**

Old Byland is a sleepy, attractive village set around a large sloping green. Here the monks of Furness Abbey settled until problems arose due to their proximity to Rievaulx Abbey. As a result they moved four miles south and established Byland Abbey (see WALK 3). Hidden away is the small church of All Saints, with some Norman work and a simple timber framed roof. Old Byland stands on a plateau with deep cut wooded valleys to all sides but the west.

After crossing the green the road becomes enclosed once more to leave the village. Just after the village sign take a bridle-gate on the left, from where a thin path doubles back to cross a curious small dry valley, before rising past a low line of limestone outcrops into trees to the other side. The path runs on beneath a wall to reach a gate out of the trees. Below, the dry valley has opened out into a deep wooded dale. **From the gate cross over a farm track to a gate opposite.** Here pause to look back to a good prospect of the village. **Head away along two hedge-sides to drop down to a gate into Callister Wood.**

A charming hollowed path descends to a footbridge out of the wood. Cross to a stile and pass through a tiny wooded corner to a kissing-gate. Behind is a small footbridge over another stream, giving access to a wide forest track. Turn left along it through Nettledale. This area is a nature reserve, the delightful string of ponds on our left being the habitat of much waterfowl. **The track emerges onto a road: turn left to soon arrive at the junction at Ashberry Farm.** This whitewashed farm makes a lovely picture, as does the chocolate box scene by the cottage at Rievaulx Bridge, just two minutes further. **Crossing Rievaulx Bridge, turn left again on the lane back to the beckoning abbey.**

Rievaulx Abbey

12

2

AMPLEFORTH

START *Ampleforth*   *Grid ref. SE 582787*

DISTANCE *3¾ miles*

ORDNANCE SURVEY MAPS
1:50,000
Landranger 100 - Malton & Pickering
1:25,000
Outdoor Leisure 26 - North York Moors West

ACCESS *Start from the village centre. There is reasonable parking along the street and on the road descending past the churchyard from the central T-junction. The White Swan has a large patrons' car park. Ampleforth is served by Helmsley-Easingwold buses.*

S Ampleforth is a charming street village sheltering under the southernmost slopes of the Hambleton Hills. It is a thriving little place, enlivened by the presence of the abbey and college (see below). Its houses line the street most attractively, some set back along a narrow strip of green. There is a Post office, fish shop, store, and two pubs: the sign outside the *White Horse* portays the neighbouring Kilburn horse (see WALK 4). A Primitive Methodist chapel of 1854 stands opposite. St Hilda's church is set back from the main street. Clearly of some age, it has a simple interior: the sanctuary features a wooden free-standing altar. Outside is a hollow topped cross shaft.

Ampleforth is best known for its abbey and college, found some distance to the east in what is a very complete community in its own right. The abbey was founded by Benedictine monks in the late 18th century, while the college is one of the country's most important Roman Catholic schools. The church was completed in 1961, and is of impressive proportions. Inside the crypt are 25 chapels. The church was designed by Sir Giles Gilbert Scott, better known for the magnificent Roman Catholic cathedral in Liverpool, of the same era.

Head left along the main street, leaving the houses behind and climbing to a brow. Just yards after a back road turns off up to the right (for Hambleton) take the narrow Westwood Lane. Already we have glorious views over the Howardian Hills. **Beyond a sawmill this loses its full surface and runs on for a considerable time as a charming, leafy lane.**

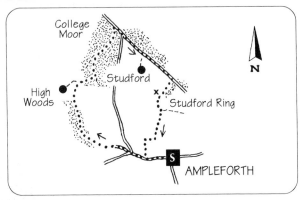

Over to the left the isolated house at High Woods comes into view. When the track drops to turn sharp left to the main beck on the approach to the house, leave it by turning right just before a tiny side-stream on the bend. Entering the stream's environs a thin path follows it up to a stile into the woods proper. A good path heads away, over a minor crossroads and up a spur to climb to join a forest road. Go left here, merging with another from the head of Royalty Slack to the left, and rising pleasantly through the woods. It then swings left to rise to join a road, though the final yards can be short-cut onto the road.

Turn right along the road, passing the Ampleforth junction and along to the drive to Studford Farm. The map indicates the presence of ancient Double Dikes crossing at right-angles, but evidence is limited to one or two faint mounds in the trees on the left. **The trees provide welcome company as we continue for a further five minutes as far as a stile on the right. Head along the narrow strip of pasture to reach Studford Ring.** This ancient earthwork, thought to have been a Bronze age fort, is in superbly preserved condition. A grassy embankment almost 60 yards in diameter, and now much decorated by thorn trees, encloses a 12ft wide ditch. The clear entrance is at our side.

Resume to the far end of the tapering pasture. Here take a stile by the left-hand gate, and head along the field-sides. At the end a track forms to turn left to a gate. Don't use it, but take a stile on the right, and head down the field-side. Ahead now we have glorious views over the Coxwold-Gilling gap and the Howardian Hills: springtime blossom or the rich hues of autumn add remarkable colour to this scene. **Beyond a gate bear gently right to a stile ahead, and then down through a paddock and past a small stable block. A brief enclosed spell follows, with the deep Smith Hill Howl down to the right. Emerging, with the rooftops of Ampleforth below, the quickest finish continues straight down the track in front, joining a drive to emerge back onto the main street.**

For a more colourful finish, take the stile immediately on the right, and take a thin path down the part-wooded enclosure. Keep straight down the side to a stile in the corner. Cross a tiny stream and advance to the fence corner just ahead. Enter by the stile and a thin, clear path now follows the stream down through a charming wooded dell. Wild garlic is in abundance, and in high summer, some rampant undergrowth. This emerges onto a back lawn: keep left with the stream to pass the buildings and out onto the western end of the main street.

*St. Hilda's,
Ampleforth*

15

3

BYLAND ABBEY

START *Wass*   *Grid ref. SE 554793*

DISTANCE *4½ miles*

ORDNANCE SURVEY MAPS
1:50,000
Landranger 100 - Malton & Pickering
1:25,000
Outdoor Leisure 26 - North York Moors West

ACCESS *Start from the crossroads in the village centre. There is limited parking on the roads heading away, notably at the foot of the Wass Bank road.*

This short walk is a delight all the way, saving the highlight for the end. It is also quite a little country pub crawl, if correctly timed!

S   Wass is a modest little village sheltering beneath the wooded slopes of the Hambleton Hills. Set around a crossroads, the central feature is the welcoming *Wombwell Arms*. Up the side road to Wass Bank is the tiny and simple St. Thomas's church, complete with a clock and little bell outside. There is also a small Post office/store.

Head up the 'no through road' leaving the crossroads opposite the pub. This quickly becomes a rough lane as it rises into a wood. On the right an old pond is passed, sadly overgrown and derelict. Just beyond, there is a fork. Use neither track but go straight ahead to a small gate into a field ('Cam Farm & Observatory'). Head away outside the wood (super bluebells), a faint trod passing beneath a bright gorse bank. The way falters at the end of the main clump of gorse. Here slant continually up to the right on a faint way to reach a stile into the wood.

The wood is entered at a hairpin bend on a forest track. The following mile, to leaving the wood, is on Forestry Commission paths: walkers are welcome, but on occasion must give way to forestry operations. **Take the right branch, whch makes a long, generally steady pull up near the top of the wood. It improves into a splendid green way to reach a junction on the wood top where a stile takes a footpath out of the trees. Don't use it, but continue on a further 150 yards, then at a fork bear left into the wood. Another delectable green way runs quickly on to reach the tower which appears only at the last moment.** This is the Mount Snever Observatory, used, as its name suggests, for housing a telescope and related equipment. Not only is the door padlocked, there's not even a way up to it without a climb!

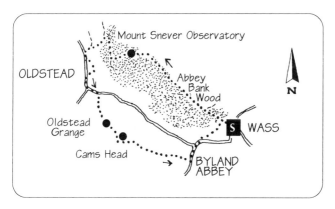

A tablet on the north side of the observatory reads

> John Wormald, in the first year of the reign of
> Queen Victoria caused this observatory to be erected

while an original inscription on the south face reads:

> Here hills and waving groves a scene display
> And part admit and part exclude the day
> See rich industry smiling on the plains
> And peace and plenty tell VICTORIA reigns!
> Happy the MAN who to these shades retires
> Whom NATURE charms and whom the muse inspires
> Who wandering thoughtful in this silent wood
> Attends the duties of the wise and good
> To observe a mean be to himself a friend
> To follow NATURE and regard his end

Leave by locating a slender path immediately beneath the corner of the tower to descend steeply through the trees. It runs clearly all the way down, hollowed and densely enclosed at the end, to debouch suddenly onto a broad forest road. Go right, then left at a junction to merge into a farm drive. Continue down to join the Kilburn-Oldstead back road, and turn left. A varied entry into the village can be made by turning left almost at once along the next driveway.

This runs to Oldstead Hall, but half-way along leave by a ladder-stile on the right. Bear left up the steep bank and then along the bank above the wood. At the top corner of the wood continue to a stile, with Oldstead's rooftops over to the right. Through this, turn sharp right to follow the hedge towards the houses. A garden corner deflects us left to a gate onto a short drive out onto the road.

Go left (passing a former chapel) to the junction at the *Black Swan*. Bear left a short way and take the first drive on the right. This leads through waving cornfields to Oldstead Grange. Pass through the farmyard, straight ahead to a gate between barns. From the adjacent stile slant down the field on a track to a bridge on a tiny stream. Across, bear sharp left on a footpath rising through trees and around the field-side. The path here has been diverted away from the house at Cams Head on the left. Advance to a fence corner and left to a stile in the corner. The way now heads along a tall, lengthy hedge-side, with the house over to the left. Gaps reveal the ruin of Byland ahead.

Over to the left the southernmost limits of the Hambleton Hills are draped in dense, mainly natural woodland. At the corner we are transferred to the other side. Two fields further (passing pig units), we abandon the tiny stream and bear straight on to find a stile beneath the lone tree ahead. Continue on to join a hedge on the left, and with the abbey just ahead now, follow this all the way along (another diversion) to emerge via a stile onto a road. Turn left to reach Byland Abbey.

Byland Abbey comprises of the abbey itself, the salubrious *Abbey Inn* (closed Mondays), and one or two dwellings. Over the side road past the inn is a 13th century gatehouse arch. The abbey is in the care of English Heritage, and an entry fee is payable to non members, though the impecunious will settle for the unhindered roadside view. It may not be Rievaulx, but there is certainly something wonderful about these Cistercian remains. Outstanding is the grandeur of the tall West

Front glowing in the evening sun as it stands high above extensive low level remains. The abbey suffered at the hands of the Scots in 1322, and was dissolved in 1538. A small museum contains interesting artefacts and information.

The founding of Byland is quite a story. The original Cistercian monks left Furness Abbey to found nearby Calder in 1134, but after Scots' raids they moved on, via York and Thirsk, to Hood, under Sutton Bank. Lack of space moved them to Old Byland, which proved too close to Rievaulx. Nearby Stocking harboured them until in 1177, after draining their chosen site, they finally settled at Byland.

Continue along the Wass road just beyond the junction, and take the first drive on the left to Abbey House. Before the buildings take a gate on the right and cross to another gate. In a larger pasture head up to the far corner to find a small gate. Bear left across to another gate and straight on to join the rough lane by which the walk began.

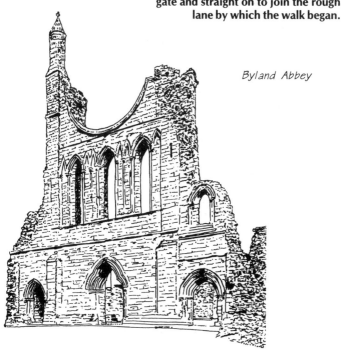

Byland Abbey

4

THE WHITE HORSE

START Kilburn   Grid ref. SE 514806

DISTANCE 6 miles

ORDNANCE SURVEY MAPS
1:50,000
Landranger 100 - Malton & Pickering
1:25,000
Outdoor Leisure 26 - North York Moors West

ACCESS Start from the Forestry Commission car park near the top of White Horse Bank, just beneath the horse itself. There is a smaller car park near the foot of the bank. Alternative starts: Sutton Bank car park, or Kilburn village. Kilburn is served by infrequent Helmsley-Thirsk buses.

A classic walk along the Hambleton scarp, and a farewell to the famous Drove Road.

S   **From the car park at the White Horse, take either the obvious path up the side of the horse, or follow the road up to its brow where a footpath sign points the way left to run pleasantly along to the top of the horse.** The White Horse of Kilburn is a landmark of Yorkshire pride, though many have only observed it from 19 miles distant, the tower of York Minster being a popular vantage point for the sharp-eyed.

This amazing creature is over 300 feet long, and was carved out of the hillside by the village schoolmaster in 1857. What sets it apart from its southern cousins is the fact that its base is not of chalk, but limestone, and consequently requires regular up-keep: visitors are begged not to walk on it. Its very size means it can only be satisfactorily seen from the vicinity of the village.

In either case this path is now followed above Roulston Scar and around the rim of the scarp. Note that young children must kept under close control above Ivy and Roulston Scars, the drop from the latter in particular being alarmingly vertical. Most visitors associate the Sutton Bank area with gliders, for here is the base of the Yorkshire Gliding Club. The clubhouse is sited just over to the right, and provides a colourful and animated scene on most weekends. The graceful movements of the gliders are often in evidence in the skies above, but more impressive still if one should be towed into the air straight over our heads when stood on Roulston Scar. It's the only way of improving on our view!

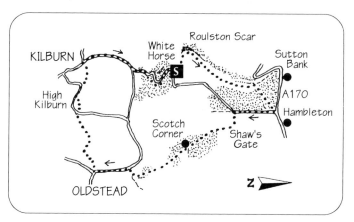

At a 'Cleveland Way' sign look back to appreciate that comment on Roulston Scar. Here our path leaves the edge by a path heading into the trees. A worthwhile extension, however, is to continue along the edge to Sutton Bank Top: even if not starting there, it makes a worthwhile detour. At Sutton Bank is the only main road to tackle the Hambleton Hills. Its reputation is now chiefly a historical one, modern cars having little difficulty - given a competent driver. Less agile vehicles can, however, still come unstuck. There are refreshments, information and parking at the top. The hairpins of the climb are seen well on the walk from Roulston Scar.

Back at the turning point, the Cleveland Way follows the line of an old dyke to emerge at a T-junction. The Casten Dyke is an ancient but clearly discernible boundary line of uncertain origin. The *Hambleton Hotel* is just a minute further along the main road. Hambleton is a renowned racehorse training area, with several large establishments nearby. **Turn right along the minor road for about ten minutes to a bend with two tracks departing the road: an adjacent track along the edge of the wood means we do not need to tread the tarmac.**

At this point only, we have good views back over our shoulder 'inland' to the moors, with the Bilsdale TV mast, Urra Moor, and the top of Easterside Hill. **At the junction take the track sharp left, which soon turns at Shaw's Gate to enter High Wood. Continue on a near-straight line along the main track which descends a little at the end of the wood. Here take a lesser track to the right to unexpectedly arrive at the chapel at Scotch Corner.**

The chapel stands in unrivalled seclusion atop the steep drop to the valley floor. It was built as a second world war memorial to Ampleforth old boys. Above the elaborately carved door is a carving of the Madonna and Child. Here in the neighbourhood of Scotch Corner was fought the Battle of Byland, when in 1322 Edward II was forced to flee from the Scots. Here also the drovers brought their cattle down off the Hambleton Hills on their long journey south, after a good 12 miles on the heights. Busier times for Oldstead!

Emergence from the trees at Scotch Corner reveals grand views of the wooded slopes of these southernmost Hambleton Hills, across to the modest Howardian Hills and more distantly the long line of the Wolds. **From a gate here a narrower path begins the descent proper. It merges into a broader track, which for a time is a delectable green way before becoming firmer to drop down through foliage, finally levelling out to join a drive and then a road at the northern end of Oldstead. The direct route back to White Horse Bank follows a pleasant, narrow back road, largely between hedgerows. More rewarding, however, is to return via Oldstead and Kilburn villages (each with a pub!)**

*The chapel,
Scotch Corner*

Turn left to enter Oldstead. This is a typical sub-Hambleton village of loosely scattered cottages. A former chapel is passed part-way along before reaching the *Black Swan* at the far end. **Just yards before the junction in front of the pub, take a gate on the right and cross a tiny enclosure to a stile. Cross straight over the field and turn left with the hedge. At the end drop round the corner to find a stile, and then slant down the gorse filled pasture to locate a sturdy footbridge over a tiny trickle. A path rises up the little bank to a gap in a tall hedgerow. Go through, and from this path junction turn right along the hedge-side.** In springtime this is a riot of colour.

St. Mary's, Kilburn

On emerging from a tighter enclosed section, slant up the bank with a hedge on the left, and cross to a gate ahead. On this grassy brow look over to the right for a classic revelation of the White Horse high above pastures and woodland. **Advance on from the gate to a small gate in a fence corner. This admits to a lovely enclosed green way, which runs on to emerge onto a back road. Cross to the gate opposite and climb the field to the stile at the top. Bear left on a pathway over the brow, and cross to a hurdle-stile in the right-hand corner. A path descends above a modern house to debouch back onto the road.**

Turn right through the settlement of High Kilburn. This consists of a scattering of attractive dwellings sat lazily back from an attractive green. **At the far end the road runs down to a sharp bend. Take the**

gate in front and head down the field on a surfaced path, with the houses of Kilburn arranged ahead. This runs on to emerge into Kilburn alongside the church, and thence the pub.

Kilburn (Low Kilburn, but not used as such) is the home of another famous Yorkshire 'pet'. The hub of the village, and open to visitors (daily except Mondays, Easter-October), are the workshops begun by Robert Thompson, the 'Mouseman', where the carved mouse climbs his furniture. This delightful trademark can be found in numerous churches, inns and houses in and beyond the county.

The village itself is also highly attractive, with a tiny beck running by well maintained cottages and gardens. In the square are the *Forresters Arms*, tearooms, and a war memorial. St. Mary's church boasts a solid 15th century tower. There is a small Post office/store on the road heading out.

Turn right through the village, keeping straight on the main road to reach the junction at the foot of White Horse Bank. En route the White Horse returns to view above us. At once the left fork begins to climb, soon entering the trees. Yards above the lower car park, a path goes off to the right. This climbs through the trees, cutting a corner then rising parallel with the road for some time before rejoining it. The main car park is to be found just a little further up the hill.

All Creatures Great and Small, at Kilburn: the carved mouse climbs another church pew, while the White Horse surveys his extensive domain

24

5

GORMIRE LAKE

START Sutton Bank   Grid ref. SE 515830

DISTANCE 5½ miles

ORDNANCE SURVEY MAPS
1:50,000
Landranger 100 - Malton & Pickering
1:25,000
Outdoor Leisure 26 - North York Moors West

ACCESS Start from the large National Park car park at the top of Sutton Bank. Seasonal bus service from Helmsley.

A spectacular walk along the Hambleton edge, contrasting with an intimate return along the foot of the scarp, deep in the woodland enshrouding Gormire Lake.

S **From the car park cross the Cold Kirby lane where it leaves the main road at the rim of Sutton Bank, and take a well worn path to the right (north). This infallible path runs along the near-level scarp, soon passing through woodland. It emerges unannounced on the very crest of Whitestone Cliff.**

This early classic is the highlight of the walk, though its sheer precipices demand that young children be kept on a tight rein. The limestone cliffs are of some immensity, and offer serious climbing opportunities. Far below, the waters of Gormire Lake repose amidst a deep bowl of greenery. Beyond it are the red-roofed villages of Felixkirk and further north, Boltby snuggled beneath the backdrop of its forest. Look back south beyond Sutton Bank to appraise the vertical plunge of Roulston Scar. Hambleton Down, on our right, once boasted a racecourse, and this is still a major racehorse training area, with several large establishments nearby.

Beyond Whitestone Cliff the way drops to a promontory before commencing a huge arc above South Woods. All this section is in clear view, and is completed far more quickly than first imagined. Just prior to the minor rise at the far end, strike off left along a sunken path to a prominent gate in the now nearby woods. A pleasant path heads away, turning to drop more steeply before a crossroads of tracks just precedes a bridle-gate out of the trees onto Little Moor.

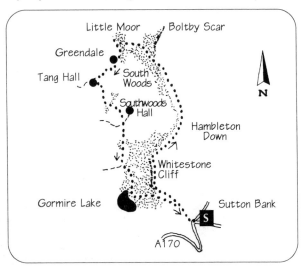

Slant down a green way to another gate to re-enter woodland. The path descends pleasantly to a T-junction of paths at a wall. Turn left through the gate and follow the fence to a gate above Greendale. Descend the field to the farm but keep left of all the buildings to a gate in a wall. A track heads through the trees past an old quarry, merging with one from the left and then joining the farm road. Note that this is a walkers' alternative to the actual bridleway, which goes round the other side of the farm and out on its drive. If in doubt, ask Pat!

Just ahead is Tang Hall, and here leave the track by turning left after the cattle-grid to a gate on the nearside of the farmhouse. A sketchy track aims half-left across the field to disappear on reaching a gate. These fields offer a splendid picture of the outward route, with

Whitestone Cliff the main feature. Peeking through the gap to the right is Roulston Scar, beyond Sutton Bank. **Head directly away from it on a faintly embanked way across a large field. Approaching a tiny plantation swing left to drop to a gate at a corner. Southwoods Hall, a curious architectural piece, is just ahead and a vague track rises to a gate in the fence in front of it. Go right with the fence to join the hall's drive, and follow it right to a crossroads of tracks at Midge Holm Gate.**

Continue straight on from Midge Holm Gate on a most enjoyable byway (former carriageway drive) between hedgerows to reach Southwoods Lodge. Here turn up to the left on a track into the woods. At an early fork go right on the main path which undulates through the woods to arrive on the shore of Gormire Lake. Gormire Lake was in view for the first mile of the walk, and eventual arrival on its shore is a lovely moment, being entirely surrounded by trees. A natural sheet of water, it lies in a deep hollow with neither feeder nor outlet. The steep return to the hilltop is along a nature trail (leaflet obtainable at the information centre).

Just beyond this point forsake the lakeside path for one climbing steeply left. It meets another path and becomes less severe to rise through the nature reserve of Garbutt Wood. At 6, note a massive, square boulder next to the path. **Eventually this excellent path rejoins, probably with some relief, the outward path on the scarp. The top of Sutton Bank is now only five minutes along to the right. On regaining the road at Sutton Bank, be sure to cross straight over to walk the few yards to the topograph - just follow the crowds.**

Whitestone Cliff, looking north along the Hambleton Hills

6

BOLTBY SCAR

START Boltby   Grid ref. SE 492866

DISTANCE 5½ miles

ORDNANCE SURVEY MAPS
1:50,000
Landranger 100 - Malton & Pickering
1:25,000
Outdoor Leisure 26 - North York Moors West

ACCESS Start from the village centre. There is some careful roadside parking. Also, outside of the village is a useful roadside parking area (east of the village, towards Sneck Yate). Boltby is served by a Monday market bus from Thirsk.

A lively climb to a delectable trod along the Boltby skyline.

S Boltby is an immensely attractive village, with tidy stone cottages under red pantile roofs. Totally uncommercialised, its enviable setting renders it near perfect. Its modest church sports a small bell-cote. A local riding school takes advantage of the many bridleways in the neighbourhood. There is also a cabinet maker's workshop here.

Leave the village centre by a 'no through road' alongside the old Methodist chapel at the very top end of the village. It winds away by ford and footbridge and eventually expires at a field. Head straight up the side, a path forming as the bracken level is reached at the foot of the wood. There is a good view back over the village backed by the extensive Boltby Forest. **Here take the broader path along to the right, quickly entering woodland. It rises, part-sunken, soon leaving the trees on the right to arrive at a junction on a little knoll.** By now we have extensive views over the plain to the eastern Yorkshire Dales. **Turn up to the left, a lovely path climbing (again part-sunken) to a gate out of the trees.**

Slant up the pasture to another gate into the edge of a plantation, then rise directly up, over a crossroads and curving up - still with the wall - to soon level out. Here the wall finally parts company and a big rock suggests a halt. Just two minutes on, however, a level walk leads to a gate out of the trees. Part-sunken yet again, a green path slants up the moor edge to gain the Cleveland Way path running along the Hambleton escarpment.

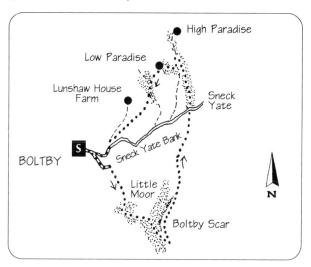

Turn left, heading north to soon arrive above Boltby Scar. Just up to the right, the prominent grassy mound in the field is the site of a Bronze age hillfort. The grand path above Boltby Scar is a splendid viewpoint, with Boltby nestling at one's feet far below; the Hambleton Hills stretching away both north and south; and on a clear day the mountains of the Yorkshire Dales beyond the flat Vale of York. There is a great sweep of moorland eastwards too, featuring the Bilsdale TV mast, the Hawnby Hills and some Tabular edges.

The Yorkshire Dales skyline from Boltby Scar

Looking back to Boltby Scar from High Barn

A brief enclosed section follows above an old quarry, beyond which remain with the wall to the prominent High Barn on the skyline ahead. A little beyond it, as the Sneck Yate road is approached, leave the wall in favour of a sketchy green way which bears slightly downhill to a gate in the wall ahead. Sneck Yate is the high point of a minor road over the Hambleton Hills, giving motorists a brief opportunity to enjoy the views we can savour for several miles. **Cross straight over the road and head along a firm woodland path. At the far end it runs on as a fine green way to join the farm road leading to High Paradise. Turn left to commence the return.**

Passing a pair of 'Legoland' cottages, turn right just beyond, down the drive to Low Paradise. Turn down to the house, using a gate at the front corner, and another in the fence just below. Descend the steep fields to a farm bridge over a small beck. Bear left into a field sometimes used as a moto-cross track, crossing to a gate near the end where wall and fence meet. Cross over the forest road and up the track behind.

Emerging at a gate follow the right-hand fence away. With Lunshaw House Farm visible up above, stay with the fence beneath a small plantation to emerge into a large pasture. Contour across this beneath a small, fenced reservoir, and keep on towards the end. Here rise to a gate onto the farm drive, and go left down it to join a road. The small, long abandoned quarry site at this corner is resplendent with snowdrops in season. **Turn right for a short five minutes into Boltby.** This road affords a near complete picture of the circuit just enjoyed.

HAMBLETON DROVE ROAD

START Kepwick   Grid ref. SE 468909

DISTANCE 5¾ miles

ORDNANCE SURVEY MAPS
1:50,000
Landranger 100 - Malton & Pickering
1:25,000
Outdoor Leisure 26 - North York Moors West

ACCESS Start from the village centre. There is a small car park adjacent to the church. If using the roadside don't encroach upon the verges.

A lovely climb to the best section of this famous old road.

S Kepwick is an unassuming little village, totally linear with wide cropped verges along the road and some lovely cottages set sedately back from it. Its modest church has a tiny bell-cote, while at the other end of the village a drive runs along to Kepwick Hall.

Leave the village by the Cowesby road past the church, and just beyond the de-restriction sign take a gate on the left. Rise by gorse bushes and a fence to a gate in the wall at the top, from where a good path climbs through the bracken. On emerging from a deep groove the hardest work is behind, and the path continues by a wall along a lovely open pasture. At the end a gate takes the wall to the other side, and our way resumes up a narrow strip of moorland-cum-scrub woodland to rise gradually higher. Curving left with the wall the path rises onto the heather moor of Gallow Hill to approach a corner of Boltby Forest.

Cross one track and within yards merge with a firmer one. Go left with it to the edge of the trees, and here take the right-hand (less steep) of two tracks rising away. Running on a terrace of sorts there are some good glimpses over the vast forest to the silhouette of Whitestone Cliff and Hood Hill. **Keep left at another junction as it rises to eventually meet another wide track at the top corner of the forest. Take the gate on the left to gain the open moor at Steeple Cross.** The stubby Steeple Cross is an old boundary marker.

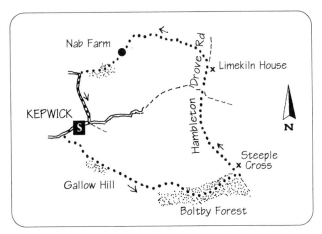

We are now on the Hambleton Drove Road, which is followed north for a mile and a half. The drove road is a classic moorland highway. Though in use probably since Bronze age times, its fame and magic spring from the busy droving days centred around the 18th century. Then it was the way of the Scottish drovers and their vast herds of cattle heading for the markets further south, avoiding the costly turnpike roads when they appeared. The drovers clung to the high Hambletons from Scarth Nick to Oldstead, though some parts are now surfaced. The remaining green road is unsurpassed for sheer atmosphere.

Glorious strides lead on over the open moorland, though the left-hand wall never leaves our side. Note the prominent burial mound of a howe over to the left on starting out. When views appear, we have Great Whernside, Buckden Pike and Penhill prominent far across the plain, with the Teesdale moors much further north. Ahead, meanwhile, on our old road is Black Hambleton, with its distinctive scarred

western flank. Set along the old road are some old boundary stones inscribed 'CT 1770'. **An old road - surfaced on the Kepwick side - is crossed amidst a barrage of notices, and the way resumes to a minor dip where a crumbling wall commences on the right.** The sparse ruins here are those of Limekiln House, a former drovers' inn.

Yards past the ruins, a gate in the wall on the left sees us heading back for the valley. A splendid green path descends with a wall through colourful terrain. Over to the left note the site of the substantial former Kepwick Quarry, while down below is the village and its lovely surroundings. **At the bottom a small new plantation sees us leave the wall to drop to a gate by an old limekiln. Just below it a beck is crossed and a firm track curves around to Nab Farm. Keep left of the buildings onto the farm road, which leads down to the Kepwick-Silton road. Turn left for a quiet final few minutes back to Kepwick.** During this stroll a glance up to the left will identify the former tramway serving the old quarry.

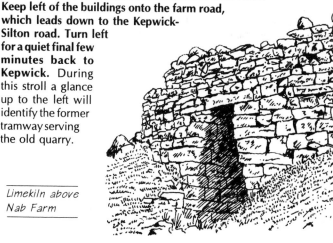

Limekiln above Nab Farm

33

8

BLACK HAMBLETON

START Snilesworth   Grid ref. SE 510944

DISTANCE 6¾ miles

ORDNANCE SURVEY MAPS
1:50,000
Landranger 100 - Malton & Pickering
1:25,000
Outdoor Leisure 26 - North York Moors West

ACCESS Start from the Hawnby-Osmotherley road just south of Low Cote Farm, Snilesworth. There is a parking area where the road - between two steep gradients - meets Wheat Beck. An alternative start is the large car park at Oakdale Head.

• IMPORTANT The opening section from the moor-gate to White Gill Head is not a right of way, but the landowner is not averse to its considerate use. Please keep to the track, don't bring dogs or large parties, and please don't light cigarettes (filthy habit anyway!). If the grouse shooting season is in full swing or at times of high fire risk, ring the estate office in advance on 01439-798380.

A grand climb to Black Hambleton and the Drove Road, almost entirely through moorland surroundings. Apart from the fine paths underfoot and the lack of navigational details, the great pleasure of this walk is the diversity of scenery, nearby and distant. At various stages all points of the compass appear, disappear and then return, but there is never a complete all-round vista. This cat and mouse game is rather enjoyable!

S The scattered community of Snilesworth stands at the very head of Ryedale: above it are only the moors. Low Cote, on a sharp bend of the road, hides the phone box and is nearest thing to a focal point.

From the car park cross the farm bridge over Wheat Beck and follow the Lower Locker Farm drive up through the field. As it doubles back up to the left, branch right through a bridle-gate. An old hollowed way slants up into a field, continuing more faintly up the wall-side to a gate onto the open moor. This is the point to which we shall return. Take the thin path climbing left near the wall. On gentler ground it bears slowly away from the wall, and before reaching the steep bank, becomes a broader way. After swinging nearer the wall again, it then turns to commence a large zigzag up the steep bank.

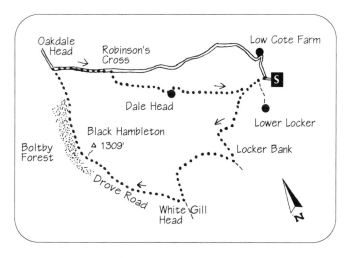

The climb is worthy of regular punctuation in order to appreciate the rapidly expanding view. Beneath is the infant Rye, wooded as ever, with patchwork fields rising to the background composed entirely of moorland. To the north is Carlton Moor, quickly joined by Cringle Moor and then Cold Moor as height is gained. Eastwards are the abrupt scarps of the Tabular Hills, while to the north-west is Beacon Hill above Osmotherley. Closer to hand, the hardy old birchwood of Bawderis Wood high on the flank of Black Hambleton is in view during the climb and much of the return. **At the top of the zigzag the moor top is gained at a T-junction. Turn right along this level track which eventually swings round to meet the Drove Road at White Gill Head.** Curiously we join it by heading south, though we are to follow it north.

Head right along the wide old highway, which with its accompanying wall rises almost imperceptibly over Black Hambleton to reach a substantial cairn. The dismal afforestation left of our path is seen to cover an enormous area. Beyond the dead-flat vale rises the long line of the Pennine Hills. At the cairn a path (no right of way) branches off for a two-minute detour to the OS column on Black Hambleton's summit. Black Hambleton is the highest and northernmost of the Hambleton Hills. Beyond the divide of Oakdale Head and upper Ryedale rise the Cleveland Hills.

From the cairn the track descends fairly rapidly. Ahead, the red roofs of Osmotherley are conspicuous. **The way levels out again to join the unfenced Osmotherley-Hawnby road at Oakdale Head.** Just before this, at a gate, we pass the inscribed Grayhall Stone, a boundary stone. **Turn right along the road, with a reasonable verge to assist.** The boundary stone of Robinson's Cross occupies the modest brow, where an improved verge takes over. **Within minutes of the brow leave the road by a good track to the right, which leads unfailingly down to Dale Head Farm.**

Turn left along the front of the house. A few years ago this was a mere shell, but has recently been renovated. **Head down the field to the beck alongside a crumbling wall. Don't use the slab bridge, but turn right between beck and wall, and when the latter ends cross the beck to a path down the opposite bank. Soon a gate is met and from it the beck is re-crossed.** Immediately beneath a confluence, this is a lovely spot for a breather. **The path then rises left back onto the moor. It soon levels out to run along to meet the moor-gate again, all the while distancing itself from the beck down to the left. At the gate on the outward leg is met, and opening steps retraced.**

The Grayhall Stone

Black Hambleton summit, looking to Carlton Moor and Cringle Moor

9

ARNS GILL

START *Snilesworth   Grid ref. SE 529928*

DISTANCE *6½ miles*

ORDNANCE SURVEY MAPS
1:50,000
Landranger 100 - Malton & Pickering
1:25,000
Outdoor Leisure 26 - North York Moors West

ACCESS *Start from the Forestry Commission's Hazel Heads car park, 2½ miles north of Hawnby on the Osmotherley road. It is simply a large roadside pasture.*

An uncomplicated circuit of a moorland side valley. Go when the heather blooms, or in the depths of winter.

S At the outset the Black Hambleton plateau shrugs its massive rounded shoulders to feature prominently across the valley. **From the car park turn along the Osmotherley road, quickly descending to cross a beck.** This is a lovely corner, deep in woodland. Over the bridge is an old limekiln. **Doubling back up the other side, the direct route remains on the narrow road until a sharp bend at the top, where the drive to Scotland Farm turns off.**

The nicer way is to leave the road half-way up, by a stile on the left some way after Street Gate Farm. Head up the left side of the field until a gap-stile in the wall. Through it, go just yards further up to a gate in the corner. Climb by the right-hand boundary to enter a short-lived, walled green way. Emerging, bear left across the stony field to a stile onto a road. Go right the few yards to the Scotland Farm drive.

Turn up the drive, but as it swings right for the farm, keep straight on a firm track to a gate and stile onto the moor. Plain sailing ensues as a long, very steady pull is made onto the broad Cow Ridge. The

track is a pleasant affair with extensive views. On the right we pass a cluster of tumuli, while on the left we pass the unmistakable site of an ancient field system. A whole network of walled enclosures remain as low rows of stones in the heather. On one or two occasions on this moorland section, the 'invisible' right of way strays slightly from the more practical line of the firm tracks. **Just beyond the old settlement the track rises to a skilfully built 6ft cairn on the knoll of Iron Howe. Beyond, resume virtually level, past a branch left after half a mile and continuing a further half mile until a tempting branch turns sharp right. Here keep straight on, the track quickly turning to descend, in winding fashion, to a wall below. Over the valley the old farm of Head House, our objective, is prominent.**

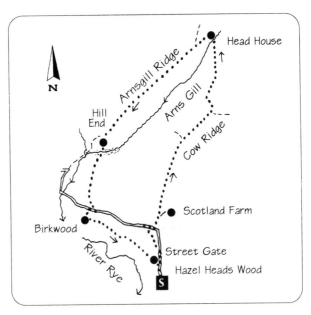

The track passes over a cattle-grid and down to the beck before climbing to Head House. It now serves only as a shooter's house, and is open for shelter from the worst of the elements. This is also the turning point of the walk. Sit on the grass here and ponder how the busy world seems a long way off... While doing just that, I was fortunate enough to be able to watch two stoats playing like kittens.

Our track resumes by slanting back up from the house to a cattle-grid back onto the moor. A delectable green track bears left, passing a cairn where a bridleway comes in, and quickly reaching a junction. Keep left along the track for a prolonged return along the west side of the valley. There are no branches, and the track eventually drops down to a gate off the moor. Over to the right on the opposite slope is Snilesworth Lodge. A couple of field-sides see us down to Hill End Farm. Turn left into the yard, and along the front of the house to a gate. Turn down the wall-side, through the reedy bottom corner to a footbridge on Arns Gill. Immediately downstream, the beck is absorbed by the Rye, itself merely an infant stream at this stage. Rise up the enclosure behind to a gate onto our final tract of moorland.

A sunken way slants up to the right, levelling to reach a wall-corner. Follow the wall until it starts to drop away, then bear clearly up to the left to resume on an intermittent, level way through heather. Approaching a fence swing left to a gate to join the road. The direct return to the left leads straight back to the start. The twin Hawnby Hills are well seen from this angle.

A far nicer return, on an old road now only a grassy way, sees us go right a few yards to the drive to Birkwood. Just a few yards further, incidentally, is a superb example of a limekiln, plum on the road-side. Descend the drive but leave half-way down by the diverted path on the left, over a stream to a stile. Turn down the field to a gate just along from the house. Go left here along a short-lived walled way. Emerging, continue on with the wall, and when a fence takes over use the right-hand gate to resume. The way remains obvious as it runs on, at times fully enclosed and between woodland, to arrive at Hagg House Farm. The entire length of the route from Birkwood back to the modern road beyond Street Gate Farm is a much older section of road. Evidence abounds, in the form of the very name *Street Gate*, and in the embanked and culverted nature of the old way. There are also occasional glimpses of paving.

Pass to the right of the house, but don't take the drive away to the left, but keep right of the barn in front to a gate into the field-top. The way resumes, largely obvious as before, including a section above South Wood. Beyond, it crosses to Street Gate Farm. Pass along the front of the house and straight out on the short-lived drive. It joins the road where we began, so retrace steps back down to the beck and up to the car park.

10

ARDEN HALL

START Hawnby   Grid ref. SE 543898

DISTANCE 6½ miles

ORDNANCE SURVEY MAPS
1:50,000
Landranger 100 - Malton & Pickering
1:25,000
Outdoor Leisure 26 - North York Moors West

ACCESS Start from the T-junction outside of the hotel. Other than
the hotel patrons' car park, parking is limited to isolated spots. A
good layby is found by the Osmotherley junction. There is also
some room by the church on the lower Kepwick road.

A lively ramble taking in many diverse features of the Ryedale
environs of Hawnby.

S   Hawnby boasts an enviable setting in the heart of upper Ryedale,
and is in fact the largest community above Helmsley. It rises steeply
from near the river up the lower slopes of Hawnby Hill, gazing across
the heavily wooded dale. The upper section includes a pub, the
Hawnby Hotel, and most of the cottages. Once a Quaker stronghold,
this quiet backwater seems to have let a few decades pass by. Set in
splendid isolation by the wooded riverbank is All Saints church, with
some Norman work. It also contains the tombs of many generations
of the Tancreds of Arden Hall. In the cluster of buildings by the bridge
is the former Wesleyan chapel of 1770, while the village Post office/
store survives in the row of cottages opposite.

**From the top of the village descend the road and cross the bridge
over the Rye. If starting from the church, just follow the level road
along to the bridge. Immediately after the kennels on the right, take
a stile and cross the field-bottom. On a small bank above a beck at**

the end, go forward to a stile onto a farm road and turn right. There are now grand view back over the Hawnby scene. **After a steepish pull it runs on towards Sunnybank farm buildings. One field short of them, take a gate on the right and up a field-side to a gate to the right of a large barn. A track rises away to the right and at another gate runs along the outside of a wood.** This and the next enclosure are currently open to visitors under the Countryside Stewardship scheme, though as footpath and bridleway already run through them, there is little extra benefit as regards access. The area is being managed in the best interests of this limestone grassland.

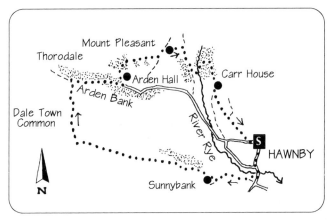

At an early opportunity fork left for better views, these twin tracks merging at a gate just before the barns of High Buildings. Here the ancient and still clearly discernible ditch of Cross Dyke is crossed. On approaching the barns, note the numerous grassy knolls on the left, the circular banks of what were probably Iron age burial mounds. **A good track continues beyond the barns, running along the field-sides to eventually reach a gate onto Dale Town Common.** This is a superb extent of open moor, made more improbable by the richly tended farmland all around. The trees ahead are the upper limit of the Boltby Forest where it encroaches on the Hambleton Drove Road.

Turn right along this short-cropped moor on a fine track. All too soon the end is reached above the deep-cut Stony Gill Hole. This makes a good foreground to a splendid view eastward to the Tabular Hills, lined up behind Hawnby Hill like a series of uniform steps. **Descend-**

ing to a gate, the track fades on the brow of a small ridge: yards further it returns to join the unsurfaced Kepwick-Hawnby road at Arden Bank. At this point we are treated to a sudden, dramatic bird's-eye view into wooded Thorodale, with its reservoir glittering amongst the greenery, and moorland slopes behind. **Head right down it, passing old quarries until it becomes surfaced at the drive to Arden Hall.**

At Arden Hall

The impressive structure of Arden Hall dates from the 17th century, and stands on the site of a Benedictine nunnery. It has charming gardens, and the surrounding woods produce a riotous display of spring flowers. **Turn down the drive and left past the hall, soon forking right after a short row of cottages. A good track drops down to a beck before rising through a wood.**

Well hidden in the private grounds is the Nuns' Well, a deep, circular, man-made pool. Water issues at one side and flows underground from the other, re-emerging just yards below. Alongside the well is a roughly carved cross. **Emerging into a clearing the track forks: take neither, but leave by a gate on the right. An invisible path runs along the bottom of two fields to join the drive to Mount Pleasant Farm.**

Go left and into the confines of the farm, keeping straight on past the buildings to a gate. Ahead, Hawnby Hill is seen side-on, looking quite substantial across the wooded Rye. **A wide track heads away, and when it swings sharp left take a stile on the right to cross a field-**

bottom to a gate. A track then runs along the edge of a lovely wood, Half Moon Plantation. Immediately after a ford take a gate on the left and recross the beck by a footbridge. Just below it the river Rye is joined and accompanied upstream as far as a footbridge.

The Rye is the major river of the western part of the Moors, flowing 16 unspoilt miles to leave the National Park at Helmsley. Several other Moors' rivers are absorbed on the flat Vale of Pickering before its own identity is lost in the Derwent, just short of Malton.

All Saints, Hawnby

A path resumes up the other bank, and after 50 yards forks as both branches leave the river to quickly rejoin after climbing through the wood. Rising to a gate, don't use it but take a path along to the right. This runs a level course through more delightful woodland to a gate out of the trees. A faint way rises to the isolated cottage at Carr House.

Pass to the right of Carr House and out along its old drive. Keep straight on to a gate in the fence ahead, and follow a field-bottom until a track materialises just prior to meeting a firmer track. Continue on this to emerge onto a road opposite Manor Farm. Turn left to re-enter the village, or right on the road which turns to descend to the church at a fork.

HAWNBY HILLS

START *Hawnby*   *Grid ref. SE 543898*

DISTANCE *5 miles*

ORDNANCE SURVEY MAPS
1:50,000
Landranger 100 - Malton & Pickering
1:25,000
Outdoor Leisure 26 - North York Moors West

ACCESS *Start from the T-junction outside of the hotel. Other than the hotel patrons' car park, parking is limited. A good layby is found by the Osmotherley junction. An alternative start is Moor Gate, where the walk crosses the Osmotherley road.*

An easy circuit of two shapely hills, with beautiful views over Ryedale and neighbouring Bilsdale.

S For a note on Hawnby, please refer to page 40. Hawnby Hill and Easterside Hill are twin-like outliers of the Tabular Hills, which occur with great regularity in a curvaceous line across the southern half of the moors. With their upturned boat appearance, these two betray their colleagues which drop steeply only to the north. **In addition to the main route, an alternative start to this walk is described on the following page. It unites with the gentler route at Moor Gate on the far side of Hawnby Hill.**

The first option is the main route, the right of way. Head west along the Kepwick road, and just opposite Manor Farm take a gate on the right to follow a farm track over several fields. Over to the left are lovely views to Arden Hall and its wooded environs (see WALK 10), while beyond, the moorland prow of Black Hambleton projects. **The track then rises a little before running below a wood to isolated Hill**

End House. Pass to its right to continue by a fence. Beyond an intervening fence a lesser path rises gently across the northern slope of Hawnby Hill to join the Osmotherley road at Moor Gate.

The second option is available while Hawnby Hill is under the Countryside Stewardship scheme. This means that access is permitted on foot to the areas indicated on the map at the entry stile. However, as these agreements are for 10 year periods only, there are currently no plans to show the areas and paths on OS maps.

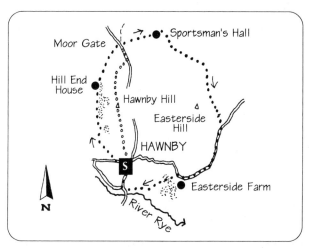

Leave the road at once by an enclosed way rising between cottages directly above the road climbing to the T-junction. At the top it emerges into a field. Rise to the top-left corner to a stile giving access to open country at the foot of Hawnby Hill. Go left a few yards to the nab end of the spur, then take the inviting path working up it. The gradients of this superb route soon ease, and gentler walking leads along the crest of the hill. Passing through a nick above Hawnby Hill Crag down to the left, the highest point is soon reached.

What a gem! .... The Ryedale scene is outstanding; Easterside Hill and Black Hambleton sandwich a rich tapestry of moorland above a gentler part of upper Ryedale. The superb habitat of Hawnby Hill is being managed to encourage heather regeneration on the northern end, and to enhance the limestone grasslands on the top and west sides. **Leave by continuing off the end (though a sunken old path may be found curving down the right flank just short of the end). Either way, bear right down the slope to a stile in the fence ahead, and continue across the moor to gain the open road. Go left the short way to the cattle-grid at Moor Gate, where the routes merge.**

Over the cattle-grid go sharp right on the drive to Sportsman's Hall. Keep left of the buildings, and level with the house go left past an outbuilding to cross a field. From the gate at the crumbling wall corner at the end turn down to the wooded bank, and descend to a footbridge on Ladhill Beck. From it bear right up the bouldery pasture, crossing a broad track to reach the wall-corner at the top.

Hawnby Hill is the finest feature of the view westward, which still features upper Ryedale running away to Black Hambleton. **From the stile a narrow path heads across the moor to a wall corner, with Easterside Hill directly ahead. The path goes left with the wall for about a mile around the northern slope of the hill, eventually descending to a stile onto a back road.** Easterside Hill overlooks the confluence of Seph and Rye in gloriously wooded surroundings.

Go right for a short and delectable road mile to Easterside Farm. Virtually traffic-free this promenade affords glorious views over the meeting of Ryedale and Bilsdale, with Roppa Edge prominent across the latter. Rounding the end of Easterside Hill, Hawnby Hill returns ahead, along with the village itself. **Immediately after the farm, take a gate on the left and drop half-right to a stile into the top of the wood. Descend a wet section to a stile at the bottom, and continue down with a tiny stream to a footbridge at the bottom. Cross it and head away, a basic track running through a couple of fields with the cottages at Hawnby Bridge just ahead. Emerging onto the junction at a gate, with the Post office/store sat in a row of cottages just ahead, the walk concludes with a steep climb up to the right.**

Left: Hawnby Hill from the south
Easterside Hill from Moor Gate

12

BILSDALE VIEWS

START *Bilsdale*   *Grid ref. SE 569920*

DISTANCE *6 miles*

ORDNANCE SURVEY MAPS
1:50,000
Landranger 100 - Malton & Pickering
1:25,000
Outdoor Leisure 26 - North York Moors West

ACCESS *Start from the lay-by at Birch Wood, exactly one mile south of the Sun Inn.*

S **From the lay-by leave the road at once by a gate into the corner of Birch Wood. A green pathway slants gently up through delightful natural woodland alongside an overgrown sunken way. Soon levelling out, this leads to a gate in the opposite corner. Cross to a track climbing the other side of the field, and follow it all the way up the field-sides to the long abandoned Carr Cote.**

Look back to savour a super scene over Bilsdale, from the dominant Easterside Hill, accompanied by Hawnby Hill and Black Hambleton. **Go left through a gate after the ruin, and across a field-side to enter a stony enclosure. At the far end look down to the left to see the scantier ruin of New House, then take the gate on the right onto the open heather moor.**

This is the vast sweep of Laskill Pasture Moor. While the untrodden footpath heads straight off, it is far better to go left along the wall-side for five minutes to join a firm shooters' track. Now go right along this for a much steadier march across the moor. The target of the near corner at Roppa Wood is soon reached. Up to the right is the long wall of Roppa Edge (see WALK 13).

Don't enter the plantation, but get your bearings and turn directly away. A contrastingly thin path, indicated by a small cairn, sets off due north back onto the moor. It is easy to locate, and is further aided by the company of a deep, dry sike. Simply forge on along this for a lengthy spell. Features of interest, other than distant views, include a curious red brick shelter over to the left, and then an impressive cross 75 yards to the right. The roughly hewn shaft has been restored to its base, and it still fulfils its use as an alms stone.

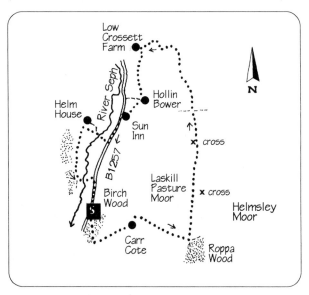

The way has levelled out by now, and gently swings right with the now shallow ditch. All around are great sweeps of rolling heather moor, and in late summer the glorious scent is a tonic in itself. **The path becomes intermittent but remains sufficiently obvious to reach another old cross on a modest brow.** This too has been restored to its base, though clearly it is a shorter version. The old shaft, in part at least, lies alongside, with an old boundary stone for company. This moment is further enhanced by the appearance of the Cleveland Hills ahead: Cringle Moor, Cold Moor and Hasty Bank are now lined up at the head of Bilsdale. The size of the TV mast can also be discerned by the scale of the attendant buildings at its foot.

A thin trod resumes north, still with a grooved way. Pass by wooden shooting butts alongside a reedy pool, and straight on to the right end of a line of stone butts. Just past them a solid shooters' track is reached (grid ref. 586935). Cross straight over and off on a clear path past a scrappy cairn, rising ever gently alongside hollowed ways. It bears left, improving into a super path.

The ground to the left falls away sufficiently to appraise a great valley scene, all the way up Bilsdale and west to Black Hambleton. The top of Carlton Moor comes in to join its colleagues, of which Hasty Bank's flat top is distinctive. North up our valley side is secretive Tripsdale, subject of WALK 15.

Some cairns mark the clear line of the path, which part way along becomes neither footpath nor bridleway, but is within the Nawton Tower access area. A glance at the map, however, shows the footpath to branch left off it, and though entirely invisible on the ground, its course slants down to a fence marking the lower boundary of the moor. Although at the time of survey there was no stile to be found, by the time of publication a brand new stile should be in evidence. Descend straight down the pasture to a gate in a protruding wall corner. Here the path yet again shuns the more inviting option, namely the hollowed way that begins to take shape down the near-side of the wall. Instead, pass through the gate and turn right with the wall along the top of a couple of fields. More new stiles may make their appearance here.

Down below, our objective of Low Crossett Farm appears, as do the vicarage and church: Fangdale Beck is there too, well sited under the moor. Advancing on across a narrow field top to the gate at the end, slant down the next field top, now with a fence for company across whihc is a bridleway on more colourful terrain. At the far corner is a gate: don't pass through, but turn left with the wall, a part sunken way running down this lush pasture. At the bottom take the left (furthest) of two gates. Head down the wall-side through colourful outbreaks of gorse to another corner gate immediately above Low Crossett Farm.

Go left on a grassy way along the back of the house. From the gate at the end head away with the fence above until reaching a stile in it. Cross straight over to a reedy corner defending a step-stile, then along to cross a section of fence in the wall in front. Now cross the bottom of the large tract of rough pasture, all the way on to join the drive at **Hollin Bower.** Note the old water troughs immediately on the left. **Cross straight over to the ladder-stile in front, and the grouping at Spout House is seen below.**

Old cross, Helmsley Moor

Waymarks see us to the wall corner just to the left, then slant down through two fields to the environs of the farm at the *Sun Inn*. Turn down to the right and pass through the yard by a series of gates to emerge alongside the inn. In fact, we emerge between inns past and present. The modern day *Sun Inn* slakes thirsts on the left, while the old pub awaits visitors on the right. The original *Sun Inn* is regarded as one of the finest examples of a 16th century crook frame cottage. The old *Sun Inn* closed in 1914, having remained virtually unaltered since the day 200 years earlier when, as Spout House, a farm tenant's cottage, it became an alehouse.

This superb old house is open to view from Easter to October, daily except Thursdays, and really does merit a visit: a guidebook can be purchased. A potter round reveals much of interest, including the old cellar which would still serve its purpose well, for on the scorching day of my visit it was refreshingly cool. To be fair, the present inn exhibited the same qualities, with the addition of some excellent ale coming out of its handpumps!

The return to Birch Wood can be made by turning left along the road, just sufficient amble to walk off any excess indulgence on the part of non-drivers. Some good verges assist in this final mile. If wanting a break from the road for half a mile, turn off at the first opportunity. A drive on the right runs to Helm House. However, after having dropped down to cross the Seph, don't follow the drive (not currently shown on OS map) up to the farm but take a gate on the left. Head straight up the field-side to a couple of barns, emerging onto a firm track coming from the farm. Go left on this, enjoying an enclosed green section. On emerging it largely fades at a gate, but keep straight on along the field bottom. Up to our right are the plantations of Helm House Wood.

Crossing a tiny stream we emerge into a larger field: contour across to a gate part way up the wall opposite. Head away with a wall, and when it turns away after an old gateway, go only a few yards further before slanting gently down to another gateway below. Immediately beneath is a footbridge on the Seph. Cross it and turn briefly upstream, then approaching a fence turn up onto a track up the field-side to emerge onto the road. Go right for the final minutes, which are dominated by the bulk of Easterside Hill.

Spout House

51

13

ROPPA EDGE

START Newgate Bank   Grid ref. SE 564889

DISTANCE 5¾ miles

ORDNANCE SURVEY MAPS
1:50,000
Landranger 100 - Malton & Pickering
1:25,000
Outdoor Leisure 26 - North York Moors West

ACCESS Start from the Forestry Commission car park at the top of Newgate Bank, on the B1257 five miles north of Helmsley. Helmsley-Stokesley Friday market buses pass by.

Roppa Edge is not named on the OS map, but is known variously as Ayton, Rievaulx and Helmsley Banks. A very straightforward walk making use of two parallel tracks. It offers extensive views over Bilsdale, few gradients, and few chances to go astray.

S Newgate Bank is a well known hill which the Stokesley-Helmsley road surmounts to leave Bilsdale for the moor edge run down into Helmsley. Without even leaving the Forestry Commission car park with its intimate parking bays, spectacular views can be enjoyed. **From the main car park return almost to the road, then take a stile on the left to follow a wide forestry track through the trees. On emerging it continues by a fence, endlessly yet imperceptibly rising over the magnificent heather of Rievaulx Moor.**

Views over the trees constantly improve as Bilsdale leads the eye to the classic Cleveland skyline of Hasty Bank, Cold Moor and Cringle Moor. Certainly, as Bilsdale gives way to the moors to its east, to Bransdale and Rudland Rigg, it engenders little doubt that the North York Moors is the greatest expanse of heather moor in England. **Eventually the track arrives at the OS column atop Roppa Edge.**

Roppa Edge is a classic example of the format of the Tabular Hills, and our outward leg runs along the top of its northward plunge: unfortunately the conifers are also a typical feature. From the top almost all of the western moors are visible, and to the right the neighbouring Tabular of Birk Nab looks highly impressive. **Just beyond the trig. point, the track runs on to meet a narrow road.** What appears to be abandoned scrap proves to be a bizarrely-sited aluminium sculpture.

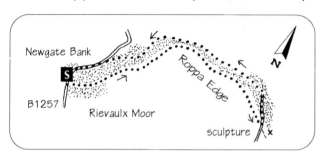

Turn left down to its demise at a crossroads of forest tracks. Head along the track to the left - it soon escapes confinement to run along the foot of Roppa Edge. This return route below the edge is a forest track which can be walked courtesy of the Forestry Commission. Only slowly do plantations return to spoil the intermittent views. **The track finally joins the B1257 part-way up Newgate Bank. Turn up as far as an old quarry.** There is a reasonable verge for part of the way, making it safe to turn and savour again the views over Easterside Hill and up Bilsdale. **At the top end of the quarry, a slender path rises above the road to reach the memorial observation platform just above.** From here Ryedale and Bilsdale fan out towards the high moors, the latter dale being especially well seen. Just below, they merge at Seph Mouth. **The car park, meanwhile, is in the trees just behind.**

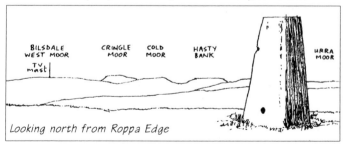

Looking north from Roppa Edge

14

FANGDALE BECK

START *Fangdale Beck*   *Grid ref. SE 572946*

DISTANCE *4¾ miles*

ORDNANCE SURVEY MAPS
1:50,000
Landranger 100 - Malton & Pickering
1:25,000
Outdoor Leisure 26 - North York Moors West

ACCESS *Start where the cul-de-sac road to Fangdale Beck leaves the main road through Bilsdale. Fangdale Beck is 3½ miles south of Chop Gate. The best parking is the lay-by outside the church on the main road, if not in church use, while there is further space by the phone box, and immediately over the bridge beneath. Friday market buses between Helmsley and Stokesley run along the main road.*

A grand moorland walk into an unfrequented side valley. A mile long section of trackless heather adds a daunting section in poor weather.

S Fangdale Beck is a lovely hamlet hidden from the road through Bilsdale. A scattering of dwellings line the tiny beck of that name. The former chapel is now a private house. The traditional green telephone kiosk by the road junction was not so long ago the subject of much furore as BT attempted to bring it up to date! Alongside the main road is the church of St. John's, Bilsdale.

Head up the road into the hamlet, keeping right when the road forks. Immediately opposite the footbridge turn right through a gate and along a drive. Follow this along the field-side until a green way comes in on the left. Here take a gate on the left and slant across the field in the direction of Stone House. Cross to a step-stile opposite and on

to a neat stepped approach to one just beyond, then continue up the field-side to a gate at the top. Here the drive is rejoined just short of the farm.

Go left along the front of the house and round the back. Ignoring a waymark straight ahead, go left through a gate between house and cottage then turn sharp right behind the cottage. Go straight up the field-side to a gate at the top, then up with the wall on the left. We are now enjoying grand views over upper Bilsdale, with Tripsdale and Hasty Bank featuring prominently. **On passing through a gateway, our way becomes a better defined sunken way.** Originally it would have been made by sledges transporting peat down from the moor.

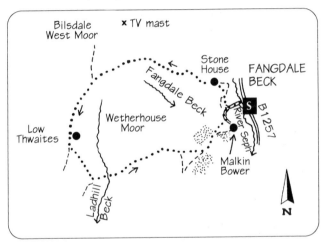

Don't rise too high with it, but bear right beneath a section of wall and alongside another section of crumbling wall: a fence also comes down here. Just past a reedy section an inviting man made way slants up the bank, escaping the bracken and climbing pleasantly towards the far wall, where it doubles back up to end by a gate in the very corner. This admits to the open moor.

A sunken way runs up the other side of the wall. Follow it left a short way then it quickly makes a pronounced swing away from the wall and onto the moor. Climb with it while it exists, then start to consider the depth of the heather. A constant distraction is the proximity of the TV mast, so close at this point. **There now follows a short mile of** trackless heather bashing, which will undoubtedly feel like a long mile! Best policy is simply to continue up the gentle slope for half a mile, then well before reaching the highest ground, bear left (west then south-west) around the very beginnings of Fangdale Beck. Soon a wall appears ahead. Approaching its corner a firm track is met. Follow this right with the wall to the corresponding corner not far ahead. Here another solid track is met coming over from the mast.

Go left along the track, declining gently in the company of the wall. It seems a little bizarre to be up on these moorland heights yet with enclosed green pastures just over a wall. Ahead, the Hawnby Hills draw attention, with Black Hambleton's vast plateau over to the right. The track remains faithful all the way down to the long abandoned Low Thwaites. Here it takes on a classy green surface, but one we shall quickly be leaving. Just yards after the wall corner beyond the buildings, take a lesser track branching left down the moor. This runs down to rejoin the wall approaching another corner. As the track bears off to the right, go straight ahead to a corresponding wall corner opposite. Just over the wall is another long abandoned ruin.

Here another good track is met. Go left along this, descending towards Ladhill Beck. At the end of the wall it swings left to drop down to ford the trickle. Just beyond, it crosses a second stream which springs up exactly on the ford. From here the way fades, and soon gives up the ghost. Simply head up easy ground towards yet another wall-corner ahead: the reedy terrain is not as it appears.

At the wall continue up on a green path that forms. At the top bear right on the old drive from Wether House, a ruin in the pasture over to the left. Within a couple of hundred yards watch for a cairn on the brow. Here the glories of Bilsdale return to the scene, beginning with an extensive moorland skyline across the valley. At the cairn turn off to the left for a short section of trackless heather, aiming towards the gap between two plantations breaking the skyline just ahead. Before reaching them a firm track is joined, this being the old road from Hawnby to Fangdale Beck. Turn left down it to a gate off the moor.

A green track descends colourful pastures featuring re-colonised quarries. After a gate by a plantation it begins a rough descent to the farm at Malkin Bower. This can be avoided by branching left down the outside of the plantation, initially steep in the rough pasture but nicer than the track. Fangdale Beck is now at our feet. From an old corner stile continue down the field-side to join the drive. Go left for two minutes back into Fangdale Beck.

TRIPSDALE

START *Bilsdale   Grid ref. SE 572961*

DISTANCE *4¾ miles*

ORDNANCE SURVEY MAPS
1:50,000
Landranger 100 - Malton & Pickering
1:25,000
Outdoor Leisure 26 - North York Moors West

ACCESS *Start from a sizeable lay-by at the entrance to the Grange, on the west side of the road 2½ miles south of Chop Gate. A Friday market bus runs through from Stokesley to Helmsley.*

• *IMPORTANT* Part of the moorland section of this walk is on a negotiated Access Area (Nawton Tower estate). Walkers are welcome subject to the moor being closed on a number of days in the grouse shooting season (commencing August 12th) and at times of high fire risk. If in doubt, contact the estate office on 01439-770012.

S **Head south along the road over the bridge, and turn left at the first opportunity up the driveway to a host of farms. Within yards turn left off this along another drive, and remain on it until it turns sharp right. Here take a gate on the left and cross the field to a footbridge on Ledge Beck.** Hard by the bridge a tiny, iron-rich spring gurgles forth. Across the beck is Hill End Wood.

In springtime Hill End Wood is an absolute carpet of bluebells, quite unsurpassed: this is Bilsdale's answer to Farndale's daffodils. **The high quality of the surroundings is echoed in the slender footpath that heads briefly upstream. It quickly turns away from the beck and climbs steeply through the wood to a ladder-stile at the top. Head up the field-side, bearing left along to a bridle-gate onto a farm drive. Go right the few yards to Hill End Farm.**

Turn right opposite the house, and on through a paddock and several gates to the end. From a step-stile on the left a path rises up the small, rough enclosure to a gateway at the top, where a larger, bracken-filled pasture awaits. Advance a few yards, crossing straight over a path between stiles either side. A little slab bridge crosses a man-made watercourse constructed to carry water for almost a mile along the hillside. Cross straight over onto a thinner path, gently through the bracken to meet one coming from the left-hand stile. This contours right to join and follow a wall. The delights of Tripsdale are laid out ahead now: the quality of our path mirrors the outstanding scenery, currently featuring some lovely woodland.

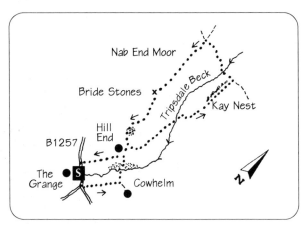

The path remains clear as it heads on through dense bracken to work down to the beck. Just beyond a gate, natural stepping stones send the path up the opposite bank, quickly becoming sunken before bending back up the steep bank. It climbs steeply through an old gateway and up to pass by an old walled enclosure. It swings left to run along as a level, grassy way, then rises a little to another gateway in an old wall, now free of bracken. From here to the top of Nab End Moor opposite, we are in the access area, though a short section in the middle is back on a bridleway. Just past here take a thinner path branching left off the rising sunken way, to run along to the crest of Kay Nest. This is a superb section, as a thin pathway runs the length of this crest. At one stage this becomes a cliff of reasonable proportions.

Beyond the end of the edge a bulldozed shooters' track is joined. Tortuous zigzags work down to the beck. Across, turn up a hollowed pathway to cut a corner of the steep, dusty climb. There are fine views right to the upper reaches of Tripsdale. **At the top things begin to ease, the track doubles back to the right, then quickly sharp left again to climb to the brow.** The view here embraces Bilsdale West Moor, Carlton Moor, Cringle Moor, Cold Moor and the Wainstones on Hasty Bank.

With a wall coming up ahead we reach a T-junction, with a boundary stone a few yards ahead. Take the inviting branch left, a super track that runs through the heather along the crest of the ridge of Nab End Moor. Just keep straight on to the beckoning cairn. Over 12ft high and boasting great valley views, it is an obvious halting place. Immediately beneath it are the Bride Stones, an ancient enclosure of upright stones. **Remain on the track (crossing a part sunken way) all the way along to a gate in the narrowing moor. Through it a green path continues on moorland, along a wall-side to the top corner of a plantation. Here a sunken way winds down the rough enclosure.**

The way doubles back to a stile into the forest. A path cuts through the corner of it, and if not impeded emerges into a field, initially still on a sunken way. Go left along the field-top to a stile at the end. If the plantation corner should be impassable, keep down the wall-side through gorse to a gate in it, then head across the large gorse pasture beneath the trees and on to the stile. **From the stile we enter the bracken pasture above Hill End again. Fork right to return to the watercourse, back through the gateway and down to the farm. This time simply follow its drive down onto the road, and go left to finish.**

Bride Stones,
Nab End Moor

ABOVE CHOP GATE

START Chop Gate   Grid ref. SE 559993

DISTANCE 3¾ miles

ORDNANCE SURVEY MAPS
1:50,000
Landranger 93 - Middlesbrough & Darlington
            100 - Malton & Pickering
1:25,000
Outdoor Leisure 26 - North York Moors West

ACCESS Start from the village centre. There is a car park at the southern end by the village hall. Chop Gate is served on Fridays by Helmsley-Stokesley market day buses.

A delightful visit to the edge of the moor, tracing the line of a spectacularly sited ancient dyke and enjoying classic Bilsdale views.

S Chop Gate (pronounced 'Yat') is, even with the support of attractive neighbour Seave Green, a small settlement, but is still a focal point in lonely Bilsdale. A major function is as a meeting point for some of the challenge walks that pass this way. The tiny Wesleyan chapel of 1858 is almost hidden at the road junction, while a war memorial stands opposite. A tablet on the school informs it was erected by the Earl of Feversham in 1909. Next door is the old school house, while a little further is the *Buck Inn*, one of only two pubs in Bilsdale. Between the two is the old smithy, bearing a lintel inscribed '1826 WR' and incorporating a horseshoe: rusting horseshoes also adorn the door. Raisdale and Bilsdale becks meet to form the Seph by the car park.

From the car park turn right, away from the village, just a few yards to the drive to Esp House. Don't use it, but take a stile on its right. Slant up to the top corner of the field to join the drive to William Beck Farm. Follow this and pass to the right of the house. Turn along to

the right, where converging walls lead to a gate. Here turn left up an enclosed green trackway. At the top continue up to the gate ahead. Looking back we have a superb prospect over upper Bilsdale and Raisdale, the skyline featuring the TV mast, Bilsdale West Moor, Carlton Moor, Cold Moor, the Wainstones, Hasty Bank. Cringle Moor appears, overtopping Cold Moor. **Now a chain of sunken ways guide the path up Black Intake to a gate onto the open moor.**

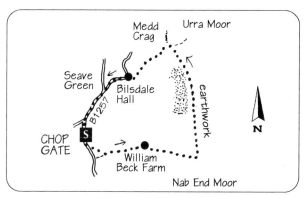

Advance just a few yards further to meet a broad trackway. Turn left along this, quickly reaching a junction above a wall corner. Go left a few yards and then as the wall descends, swing right as the track follows the beginnings of the clearly discernible line of the old earthwork. Of unknown - possibly Celtic - origin, this ancient earthwork of ditch and bank runs for three miles, generally still very clearly along the rim of the steep drop from Urra Moor to the valley.

At the end of the plantation below is a wayside boundary stone, and a deep sunken way climbing out of the end of the trees. Continue on, enjoying first-rate views and easy walking to another junction marked by a Nawton Tower estate notice affixed to a boulder. This is the point where we leave the dyke, and soon the moor. Turn sharply down to the left, and Chop Gate and its environs are revealed ahead. A sunken way winds down to a gate and stile off the moor. The track remains clear down through bracken then a reedy pasture, to run on above a tree-lined beck. At the end it swings round to emerge at the front of Bilsdale Hall. Turn down the quiet back road into Seave Green, crossing the beck to join the main road. Go left to finish, with a footway to assist the final steps.

THE WAINSTONES

START *Chop Gate   Grid ref. SE 559993*

DISTANCE *7½ miles*

ORDNANCE SURVEY MAPS
1:50,000
Landranger 93 - Middlesbrough & Darlington
1:25,000
Outdoor Leisure 26 - North York Moors West

ACCESS *Start from the village centre. There is a car park at the southern end by the village hall. Chop Gate is served by Friday market Helmsley-Stokesley buses. An alternative start is from Clay Bank Top, near the end of the walk.*

The traverse of Cold Moor's heather ridge upstages even the famous Wainstones.

S For comment on Chop Gate, please refer to page 60. **From the car park head north along the road into Chop Gate and turn left along the road to Carlton, leaving it at once up a track behind the house on the right. This is Cold Moor Lane which leads unerringly, in mixed fashion, to the moor of the same name. From the moor gate keep to the path climbing by the right-hand wall. After levelling out it begins to slope up the moor, leaving the wall at the start of a plantation. This excellent path rises seemingly endlessly at an ideal gradient to eventually join a wide track on the moor top. It is now followed right along the best and narrowest mile from the distinctive mounds of Three Howes to the top. This trek along the crest of Cold Moor neatly culminates in the summit, at its northernmost point.**

Both Cold Moor and Hasty Bank fall away steeply to the north, with dark plantations rising far too high up these slopes. Along the top of the trees runs the former jet miners' track. Jet was once a popular ornamental stone. Along with jet, these hills were also plundered for alum and ironstone. Evidence of the old workings abounds: for good examples, look at Cringle Moor from Cold Moor - just locate the right contour!

Arrival on a popular highway at Cold Moor's summit cairn is emphasised by the appearance of a stone flagged way. This will remain underfoot for the greater part of the walk to Clay Bank Top. Whilst it might well have been necessary to repair the steeper sections on and off the tops, many who love these hills have expressed dismay at the flagging of the entire high level sections, regardless of the condition of the path. **Turn right to commence a rapid descent to Garfit Gap. Ahead, the Wainstones arouse anticipation, and the path quickly climbs again to the rock pinnacles.**

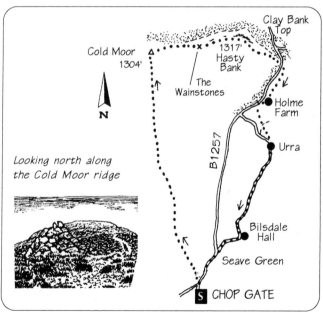

The Wainstones are Hasty Bank's pride and joy, a tumbled group of crags and boulders guaranteed to rejuvenate the most ancient of us. Climbers also play here. **The path picks an easy way between the boulders before crossing Hasty Bank's lengthy top.** Hasty Bank is not the highest point on the Cleveland ridge, but is arguably the finest. The splendid path clings to its northern edge, with the Cleveland plain contrasting sharply with the length of Bilsdale stretching away almost infinitely to the south.

Cold Moor
from Cold Moor Lane

Towards the end the cliffs on the left are of a serious scale, emphasised by the unbroken fall from just off the path. **The descent is again steep, beginning at the end of the cliffs and dropping down to join a forestry track at a stile. Instead of following this track the path continues straight down by the wall to emerge onto the road at Clay Bank Top.** Refreshments are often available at this major gap in the Cleveland Hills.

Take the gate on the opposite side, but then ignore the main path rising away from it, and instead take a gate on the right to commence the descent into Bilsdale. A green track runs pleasantly down beneath a plantation to reach Holme Farm. Go right along its drive to regain the main road.

Hasty Bank from Cold Moor

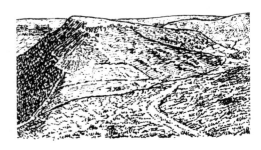

The Wainstones, looking to Cold Moor

After a mere 20 yards or so vacate the road's grass verge at a stile to descend to a footbridge. Turn downstream a short way on a briefly flagged path, then cross the field to a gate in the fence ahead. Accompany the right-hand fence, using a stile part-way along to resume on its other side. At the end take a stile behind a drive and follow the short-lived plantation fence away. From the corner slant up to the top corner of the field, aiming for the farm at Urra. Two stiles see us onto the road there.

Look back to a skyline most appropriate in view of our walk: a fine array of Hasty Bank, with the Wainstones silhouetted, and to its left, the full length of Cold Moor. **Go left on this traffic-free back road through the farming hamlet of Urra. A gradual descent is made into Seave Green. En route, St. Hilda's church is passed. On rejoining the main road go left to finish, making use of the adjacent footway.**

St. Hilda's, Seave Green

18

BILSDALE WEST MOOR

START *Chop Gate*   *Grid ref. SE 559993*

DISTANCE *5½ miles*

ORDNANCE SURVEY MAPS
1:50,000
Landranger 93 - Middlesbrough & Darlington
*   100 - Malton & Pickering*
1:25,000
Outdoor Leisure 26 - North York Moors West

ACCESS *Start from the village centre. There is a car park at the southern end by the village hall. Chop Gate is served on Fridays by Helmsley-Stokesley market day buses.*

An initial steep pull and a quiet lane sandwich a superb walk along high moorland tracks.

S For a note on Chop Gate please refer to page 60. **Leave the car park not by the entrance, but by an enclosed track climbing steeply from the opposite end. Entering a large pasture continue straight up, either in or alongside a classic sunken green way.** A rapidly unfolding view over much of Bilsdale culminates in a fine Cleveland Hills skyline, featuring Carlton Moor, Cringle Moor, Cold Moor, Hasty Bank and Urra Moor. **Above a line of spoil heaps the way runs to a stile onto the foot of the moor proper. Sunken again, it works quickly up the moor, with the top of a plantation just over to the left.**

Our good path rises gently past some butts to the prominent Cock Howe on the moor top. Now on the main ridge, we have earned views west to Black Hambleton and beyond to the Pennines, stretching from the Yorkshire Dales up into Teesdale and the North Pennine heights. Both Cock Howe and forthcoming Green Howe are well defined mounds - even without their stones - and like countless others on the moors are likely to be the burial sites of ancient chieftains. On a more modern note, the tall TV mast is closer than usual on this walk, being a mile and a half south of Cock Howe on the ridge.

A few yards beyond Cock Howe a wider track runs along the broad ridge: this is now followed to the right. Approaching Green Howe is a sudden revelation of the industry of Teesside between Carlton and Cringle Moors. **Just past Green Howe a superior track is joined. Turn right to decline steadily down Barker's Ridge.** With such easy walking, savour to the full this magnificent panorama. A pleasant surprise comes when the improbable profile of Roseberry Topping slots into the Cringle-Cold Moor gap. Another sudden appearance is that of Scugdale down to the left. Ahead is the mile-long line of Barker's Crags beyond Scugdale Gate, and the unmistakable contour-perfect piles of spoil from the former jet mines.

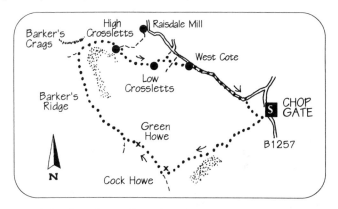

The path finally swings right to drop down to a gate where it vacates the moor. While the track descends fields to High Crossletts Farm, cling to moorland a little longer by staying outside the wall until the track there becomes enclosed at a gate in a reedy corner. Take a stile on the right and cross to the rear of the farm. From the stile drop down the near side of the house to follow the drive away.

For a simpler finish follow this down through Raisdale Mill and out onto the lane, there going right for Chop Gate. **For greater interest, go only a few yards down the drive and take a stile on the right. Cross** the field-top to a ladder-stile then turn down the field-side to a gate across the bottom. Slant down to a gate in the far corner and turn down by a tiny stream, a nice wooded corner. This increasingly pleasantly course leads down to a grassy crossing of the beck. In a leafy corner, with much holly in attendance, head along to Low Crossletts Farm.

Keeping left of the buildings head out on the drive and over Raisdale Beck. A steep pull leads onto the road, but a corner of this can be cut by branching right part-way up and crossing to a gate in the nearby wall. Follow a wall away to a gap-stile hidden in the corner to join a farm drive. Cross straight over the farm drive and slant up towards the farm buildings ahead at West Cote. Another hidden stile in the descending hedge gives access to the buildings. Pass outside the front of two houses to reach a gate into the farmyard, and turn straight up to join the road. Turn right for Chop Gate, whose red roofs soon appear ahead.

On crossing a tiny stream, conclude by taking a stile on the right and tracing the stream down to enter Raisdale Beck. Now accompany the main beck downstream in nice surrounds to a stile back into the car park.

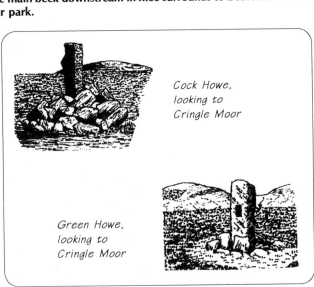

Cock Howe,
looking to
Cringle Moor

Green Howe,
looking to
Cringle Moor

19

ROSEDALE INCLINE

START Clay Bank Top   Grid ref. NZ 571035

DISTANCE 8 miles

ORDNANCE SURVEY MAPS
1:50,000
Landranger 93 - Middlesbrough & Darlington
             94 - Whitby
1:25,000
Outdoor Leisure 26 - North York Moors West

ACCESS Start from the Forestry Commission car park at Clay Bank
Top on the B1257 Helmsley-Stokesley road. It is served by Friday
market buses. An alternative start at Ingleby Bank car park (GR
578038, near end of walk) gets all the climbing done at one go.

A famous climb to the moors summit, and a descent along an equally
renowned old railway track.

S Clay Bank is the steep climb taken by the busy B1257 from the
Cleveland plain, through the pass and down into Bilsdale. The
magnificently sited car park, virtually at the top, allows motorists to
survey a sweeping panorama featuring Roseberry Topping's unique
profile from their car doors. Refreshments are often available here.

**From the car park head up the road to the brow of the hill, and take
the gate on the left. From it a wide path rises fairly steeply at first and
then very gently through the heather of Urra Moor.** The track passes
innumerable cairns and boundary stones. Across to the east can be
seen the dead straight climb of the old incline railway, soon to be our
route. **After a mile and a half the Ordnance column on Round Hill
is reached, only a few yards left of the path.** Urra Moor is the highest
of the North York Moors, and not surprisingly its view is largely of
rolling moorland. The summit is known as Round Hill, a fitting name

for this pronounced mound which is the site of a tumulus. It stands some yards back from the path, and appears to have received few visits from the hordes who pass this way on the many long-distance or challenge walks drawn to the high moors. Go seek its solitude!

The path forges on, avoiding any branches until it merges with a former railway track whose course can clearly be discerned well before it is reached. Since Round Hill the scene ahead has been one of layer upon layer of heather-clad moors, the high central ridge of the Cleveland Dome. East of Round Hill the Cleveland Hills perform a sharp dog-leg and head due north. Little else changes however, for the steep west/north scarp remains intact, with undulating moorland above and the flat plain below. Also still very much in evidence is the afforestation cloaking the steep lower slopes, seen nowhere better than on this circuit of the deep enclave of Greenhow Botton.

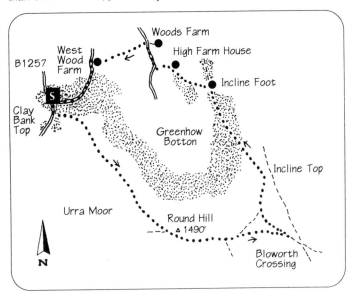

Turn left along the track bed to soon arrive at the Incline Top. The old railway line was built in 1861 to convey ironstone from Rosedale in the heart of the moors to the furnaces on Teesside. Trains crossing the moorland at 1300ft must have made an inspiring picture indeed, but possibly the line's most fascinating feature was the incline which lifted it onto the moor top. A climb of 750 feet was achieved within a mile, and our walk takes in the full length of the incline. The drum house at the top was recently dismantled. Although the line closed in 1929, this is one course that won't fade into oblivion.

Now descend the incline in low gear, at the very bottom merging with a forest road. Continue along it for a few minutes to the cottages at Incline Foot. Opposite these leave the track - now a firm drive - by a stile on the left, and slant down the field to the right corner of a wood. Go right through a gateway and along the ditch-side, becoming enclosed by a sike and a hedge on what is a lovely section. At the end, at another wood corner with High Farm House just ahead, slant down outside the wood to a stile onto the drive. Go left along it to climb away and run out to join the shared farm road in Ingleby Botton.

Go right a few minutes as far as the drive to Woods Farm. Immediately opposite, take a gate on the left and head straight across the fields, aiming for West Wood Farm backed by Hasty Bank. Entering the farm confines, the path has been diverted from that shown on older maps. Turn right in front of the main buildings and out along a short drive to the right to join a road. Turn left and within minutes the road reaches the forest, passing Ingleby Bank car park before climbing steeply to return us to the Clay Bank car park back on the main road.

Looking down the incline

20

URRA MOOR

START Clay Bank Top   Grid ref. NZ 571035

DISTANCE 5 miles

ORDNANCE SURVEY MAPS
1:50,000
Landranger 93 - Middlesbrough & Darlington
1:25,000
Outdoor Leisure 26 - North York Moors West

ACCESS Start from the large Forestry Commission car park at Clay Bank Top on the B1257 Helmsley-Stokesley road. It is served by Friday market buses.

A simple moorland triangle on good tracks, visiting the summit of the moors and tracing the line of a spectacularly sited ancient dyke.

S Clay Bank is the steep climb taken by the busy B1257 from the Cleveland plain, through the pass and down into Bilsdale. The magnificently sited car park, virtually at the top, allows motorists to survey the plain and unmistakable Roseberry Topping from their car doors. Refreshments are often available here.

From the car park head up the road to the brow of the hill, and take the gate on the left. From it a wide path rises fairly steeply at first and then very gently through the heather of Urra Moor. The track passes innumerable cairns and boundary stones. Across to the east can be seen the dead straight climb of the old incline railway, visited on WALK 19. **After a mile and a half the OS column on Round Hill is reached, only a few yards left of the path.** Urra Moor is the highest of the North York Moors, and not surprisingly its view is largely of rolling moorland. The summit is known as Round Hill, a fitting name for this pronounced mound which is the site of a tumulus. It stands some yards back from the path, and appears to have received few visits from the hordes who pass this way on the many long-distance or challenge walks drawn to the high moors. Go seek its solitude!

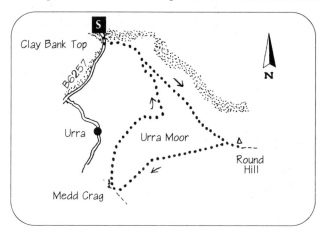

After a suitable sojourn retrace steps a few yards to a major path junction, and here leave our earlier course by forking left. This equally wide track descends steadily towards the moor edge, reaching a junction marked by a Nawton Tower estate notice affixed to a boulder. Here, as the route to Seave Green prepares to drop more steeply off the moor, turn right on a clear path. This now traces the very prominent bank and ditch of an earthwork, initially above the modest outcrops of Medd Crag. Of unknown - possibly Celtic - origin, this ancient earthwork runs for three miles, generally still very clearly along the rim of the steep drop from Urra Moor to the valley.

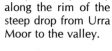

Looking back to Hasty Bank from the climb onto Urra Moor

Looking west
from Round Hill

Carlton Moor   Cringle Moor   Cold Moor   Hasty Bank

The Hand Stone,
Urra Moor

A wall soon comes up to join the path, and when it parts company the path continues along the top of the dyke. Once the accompanying wall departs beyond Medd Crag, note the bird's-eye view of Urra, and more distantly a prominent needle protruding from the Wainstones on Hasty Bank. **Maintain this course for another good mile, rising gently after crossing a beck to eventually meet the wide path coming up from Clay Bank Top. Turn left to conclude the walk as it began.**

The earthwork
on Urra Moor,
looking to
Hasty Bank

21

MOUNT GRACE PRIORY

START *Osmotherley*   *Grid ref. SE 456972*

DISTANCE *2½ miles*

ORDNANCE SURVEY MAPS
1:50,000
Landranger 99 - Northallerton & Ripon
1:25,000
Outdoor Leisure 26 - North York Moors West

ACCESS *Start from the village centre. There is ample roadside parking. Osmotherley is served by Northallerton-Stokesley buses.*

Merely a stroll through the fields, but a magnificent objective.

S Osmotherley has a highly attractive village centre which remains unaffected by more recent housing additions. A small green marks the meeting of roads lined by stone cottages, the main street sloping throughout its length. On the green is a sturdy market cross, next to which is a stone table where Wesley once preached: just around the back is his early Methodist chapel of 1754. The Primitive Methodist Chapel of 1891 is now a garage. Almost everything has a central position, with the church of St. Peter with traces of Norman work, and three inns included. Osmotherley has that 'ramblers' atmosphere not found everywhere. There are also tearooms and a fish shop.

Head up the main street (North End) as far as a rough lane (Grant Close) on the left. Head along to the end, where a kissing-gate admits to a field. Keep straight on a couple of field-sides to emerge onto a farm drive by a play area. Head along the drive to the end, where it splits into two parallel drives. Take the first one which runs along to Siddle Farm. Keep left of the buildings and on through a gate, then follow the field edge ahead to a stile at the end. This is the point to which we shall return after a visit to Mount Grace.

For now then, turn down the field-side to a stile into the woods. A good path slants down to the right, and at the wood bottom it runs along to the right before being transferred into a field (this section has been diverted). Resume along the field-side outside the wood to a stile into the priory car park. I'll leave you to look around.

Mount Grace Priory occupies a setting of profound tranquillity, nestling as it does beneath a wooded bank of the Cleveland Hills. Founded as late as 1398, it enjoyed less than 140 years of monastic privilege before the Dissolution. The Carthusian monks who lived here were a breed apart from most of the other orders: their hermit like existence was made 'easy' by virtue of their individual cells arranged around a great cloister. Of particular interest is a reconstructed cell, giving a modern insight into how these monks lived. At the entrance to the priory is the imposing guesthouse, which now houses an exhibition. The priory is owned by the National Trust and managed by English Heritage.

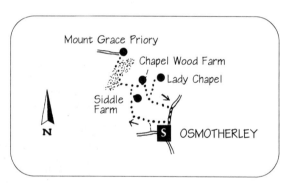

To return, head back up through the wood, and this time keep straight on up the field-side. A track forms to rise up and along to Chapel Wood Farm. Entering its confines, follow the waymarks up past the buildings to join its drive. Turn right along this, Ruebury Lane, which lead unfailingly back to the village.

Extensive views look out over the vale to the Pennine hills. **Part-way along, at a view indicator, a drive doubles back up to the left. It is only a short detour up here to visit the Lady Chapel. At the end a few steps lead up onto the chapel green.**

This lovely spot has been a place of pilgrimage for 600 years. Its bare stone walls exude a simple yet moving atmosphere that belies the modernity of the present building. A rough block of stone serves as the modest altar, while a statue in the corner depicts Our Lady and the infant Jesus.

The site is indelibly linked with Mount Grace Priory, for the Carthusian monks were drawn here by the shrine to Our Lady. At the Dissolution in 1539, the last prior came to dwell in this hermitage. It later fell into ruin, but the tradition was restored when Franciscan friars came to Osmotherley in 1665 and again catered for pilgrims. This link ended in1832, but they returned again in 1969. The chapel was rebuilt as recently as 1960, and weekly Masses are held here.

Back on Ruebury Lane, enjoy better views in to the moors, with Black Hambleton rising impressively above Osmotherley's rooftops. At the end turn right down the road to finish.

Mount Grace Priory

22

BEACON HILL

START Osmotherley   Grid ref. SE 456972

DISTANCE   7 miles

ORDNANCE SURVEY MAPS
1:50,000
Landranger 93 - Middlesbrough & Darlington
            99 - Northallerton & Ripon
            100 - Malton & Pickering
1:25,000
Outdoor Leisure 26 - North York Moors West

ACCESS Start from the village centre. There is ample roadside
parking. Alternative starts: Sheepwash or Chequers. Osmotherley
is served by Northallerton-Stokesley buses.

A look at Osmotherley's two dales, with profuse woodland interspersed with reservoirs, moorland and easy tracks.

S Osmotherley has a highly attractive village centre which remains
unaffected by more recent housing additions. A small green marks the
meeting of roads lined by stone cottages, the main street sloping
throughout its length. On the green is a sturdy market cross, next to
which is a stone table where Wesley once preached: just around the
back is his early Methodist chapel of 1754. The Primitive Methodist
Chapel of 1891 is now a garage. Almost everything has a central
position, with the church of St. Peter with traces of Norman work, and
three inns included. Osmotherley has that 'ramblers' atmosphere not
found everywhere. There are also tearooms and a fish shop.

**Leave the village centre by the Swainby road which climbs due
north. When the houses peter out take a rough road (Ruebury Lane)
to the left. It rises a little before contouring around the hill to Chapel**

Wood Farm. En route an early detour can be made to visit the Lady Chapel: see WALK 21. **As a field-track it remains level to enter South Wood. Take the right fork for a substantial climb to the moor-edge: a wall is then followed to the BT station.** If previously unaware of the presence of this monstrosity, it imparts a mighty shock on emerging from the trees next to it. **Just beyond and over the wall is the Ordnance Survey column atop Beacon Hill.**

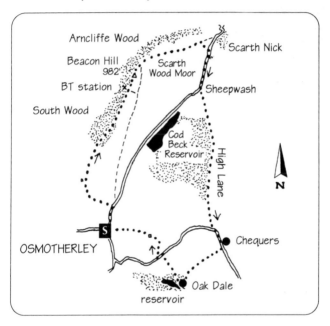

The highlight of arrival on Beacon Hill is the view north-eastward to the inspiring line of Cleveland Hills stretching away to the distant Roseberry Topping. The triangulation column on Beacon Hill is one of the best known of its kind. Here the (in)famous Lyke Wake Walk begins its march to the sea, while the Cleveland Way and Coast to Coast Walk follow more sensibly in its wake.

From Beacon Hill the enclosed path drops down to a corner of Scarth Wood Moor, a classic heather tract in the care of the National Trust. Take the main path diagonally over the moor to meet a wall

The Cleveland Hills from the path onto Scarth Wood Moor

at the far corner. Fork right at the drop to Scarth Nick to join the road just above, then turn right to reach a footbridge and ford at Sheepwash. Sheepwash is a popular picnic venue for car-borne visitors. **A rough track climbs steeply away from the bridge before levelling out to run for a good mile, becoming surfaced prior to meeting the Osmotherley-Hawnby road.** Our track from Sheepwash to Chequers is the old drove road, still unsurfaced until near the farm. It runs for many miles along the very crest of the Hambleton Hills immediately south of here, and several other walks in the book take in sections of it. North of Sheepwash it climbs from the plain to the hills through Scarth Nick.

Turn left as far as Chequers. Chequers Farm at Slape Stones was once an inn serving the drovers: note the sign affixed to the outside wall. Refreshments can still be enjoyed here, and there is a farm shop. **Yards beyond it take a track to the right by a wall. When it turns off to the left the path becomes clearer to descend through the bracken in a direct line, continuing beyond a gate to arrive at the renovated Oak Dale Farm.**

At Scarth Nick

On Beacon Hill

Upper reservoir, Oakdale

At Oak Dale a water authority road is joined. Oakdale cuts a deep course into the shoulder of Black Hambleton to the south-east. If time is not pressing, a short walk up the water authority road leads to the upper reservoir, a very colourful scene. **The main route descends to the right down this rough road, past a sheltered corner of the lower Oakdale reservoir and steeply up onto a lane. A few yards to the left take a farm drive right: it is left very briefly to use a stile beyond a gateway, then rejoined to descend to White House Farm.**

Keep right of the buildings and slope across the field, crossing a track at the bottom beyond which is a footbridge over Cod Beck. A steep climb up the wooded bank deposits us in a field with Osmotherley just in front. A couple of fields are crossed to a snicket onto a lane. Take the private-looking snicket opposite to emerge in novel fashion into the village centre.

Osmotherley

81

23

WHORLTON CASTLE

START *Swainby*   *Grid ref. SE 477020*

DISTANCE *4¾ miles*

ORDNANCE SURVEY MAPS
1:50,000
Landranger 93 - Middlesbrough & Darlington
1:25,000
Outdoor Leisure 26 - North York Moors West

ACCESS *Start from the village centre. There is ample parking alongside the beck. Swainby is served by Northallerton-Stokesley buses.*

This gentle walk might well be subtitled the *Bluebell Way*, such is the profusion of these endearing springtime blooms.

S Swainby is a delightful village centred on the stream running its entire length, and overlooked by massed ranks of high woodland. Almost all the houses line one side of the village. Remarkably there are three pubs here, along with a Post office/shop and toilets. The church of the Holy Cross stands imposingly in the centre, its tall spire overtopping all. Also gathered around are the former Whorlton Parochial School of 1856, and the Whorlton Recreation Rooms of 1919, now the village hall. Of further interest is an old roadsign by the bridge outside the *Blacksmiths Arms*.

Head up the High Street from the bridge, past the church on the other bank and eventually out of the village beyond the *Miners Arms* and the school. Past the Scugdale turning, the road rises gently as Shepherd Hill before swinging right. Here go straight on up a cart-track, which maintains the steady rise to enter Clain Wood. Turn sharp left on the route of the Cleveland Way, and a grand path runs along the edge of the wood. Entering deeper woodland, the first of

the promised bluebells leap into action. Keep on this way until a stile on the left. Ahead over the fields are lovely views into Scugdale, driving a deep wedge between Live Moor and Whorlton Moor. **Descend the field, bearing right of the trees to join a track at the bottom. This descends to a ford and footbridge, and up onto a lane. Go left to climb to Huthwaite Green.**

Scugdale was mined for jet and ironstone, with rails laid to take the latter out of the valley. Looking up the dale, note the extensive line of spoil heaps on the opposite hillside, indicating the contour of old workings. The mineral line that served the ironstone mines came down to the road junction at Huthwaite Green by the same route as we leave it. Huthwaite Green's entertainment value is limited to what can be done in a phone box.

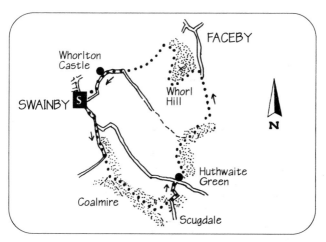

At the T-junction leave the road by a fenced path rising to a wood. At the top note the grassy embankment of the old tramway scaling the slope in front. **Our way runs to the left to a corner of the wood. Don't follow the main path over the stile into the trees, but take the gate in front and head along the field-top beneath the wood. At the end a gate sends a path into the trees, rising quickly to join a forest road. Turn left along this as far as a hairpin bend.** Stay on this for a short-cut to Whorlton Castle. A Whorlton/Faceby boundary stone stands just ahead.

Keep straight on through the old gateway on a broad track. This quickly forks: take the left branch slanting down to leave the wood. Maintain the slant down the field to a gate onto the broad track of Bank Lane, and an inviting seat. To our left rises the modest, tree-capped Whorl Hill: there is more to it than meets the eye. **Turn down the track leading to Faceby. Unless desperate for the pub, however, don't follow it all the way.**

Faceby is a cosy little village, like its many sub-Cleveland Hills colleagues 'ripe' as a dormitory for Teesside. It features the modest church of St. Mary Magdalen, with a small bell turret; the *Sutton Arms*; and a mix of attractive cottages and modern dwellings. If succumbing (you'll miss the best bit though!) turn left on entering the village along a grassy bridleway to emerge at the church. A pathway runs on to the left along the front of a house. Cross diagonally over a field (nasty bog in the centre) into a corner of the wood. Head away past a series of poultry sheds to join the main route at the far corner of the wood.

Back on the main route, meanwhile, at the first house on the left the wooded slopes of Whorl Hill begin. Take a stile and cross the edge of the lawn to a stile into the corner of the wood. On a bright, spring day, the carpets of bluebells throughout these woods are quite peerless. **Take the path climbing straight up the side of the wood. Part-way up it merges into a broader green track. Continue up until it levels out at a junction with a similar track. While one could go right, the finest way is along to the left.**

This quickly narrows into a delectable green footway, and runs all the way round the edge of the wooded slopes. The finest part is yet to come however, for rather than leaving the bluebells behind, it meanders through the most beautiful walking imaginable. In addition to all this, we also find open views out to the villages of the plain. **At the end it drops down to meet the direct branch, descending together to arrive at the opposite corner of the wood.**

Whorl Hill from Coalmire

Take the stile in front and go left on a briefly enclosed way above a house. Emerging, keep straight on the field top to a stile at the end (not the gate). This sends us along a field-side with Whorlton Castle ahead. At the end, follow the farm track across a paddock to emerge onto Whorlton Lane. Bear right, passing both church and castle.

At first glance the church of the Holy Cross appears intact, but soon proves otherwise. It dates back to the 12th century: while the chancel and 600 year-old tower are preserved, the arches of the nave stand forlorn. The chancel is viewed through a window in the door, finest feature being a wooden recumbent effigy of Nicholas de Meynell of Whorlton Castle, who died in 1322. A replacement church was built in 1877 in Swainby. Local pride maintains the old church, and a few services are still held. It is scheduled for renovation when funds allow.

Whorlton Castle's site was occupied by the Romans, whose coins and pottery have been unearthed locally. The present remains are the Meynell's 14th century castle. The gatehouse is most impressive as we approach, and bears the arms of the Meynells, Greys and Darcys. The castle has a link with Mary, Queen of Scots, for Lord Darnley's family owned it at the time of their marriage; it later saw Civil War action.

Leaving the castle, Swainby appears just minutes ahead. Reaching the edge of the village, a footpath finish can be made by taking a stile on the right and following an enclosed path along a tiny stream-side. Part-way on it crosses the distinct course of the old ironstone railway serving Scugdale. **The path emerges back onto the street adjacent to the *Black Horse*, nicely placed to begin your pub crawl!**

Whorlton Castle

24

CARLTON MOOR

START *Carlton Bank   Grid ref. NZ 523030*

DISTANCE *7 miles*

ORDNANCE SURVEY MAPS
1:50,000
Landranger 93 - Middlesbrough & Darlington
1:25,000
Outdoor Leisure 26 - North York Moors West

ACCESS *Start on the summit of the Carlton-Chop Gate road above Carlton Bank. There is a hidden car park just south of the brow.*

Verdant Scugdale separates two superb moorland sections. Whilst the moors are unsurpassed in late summer, there is much to be said for doing this walk in springtime to savour Scugdale at its best.

S The summit of Carlton Bank has altered in recent years with the provision of a cafe and car park. Though welcomed by us all, the cafe is a particular boon to long distance walkers. It offers the only on-route refreshment to Cleveland Wayfarers between Osmotherley and Kildale; and to Coast to Coasters between Ingleby Arncliffe and Blakey.

From Carlton Bank leave the road by the wide track commencing by the wood and rising towards the HQ of the Newcastle & Teesside Gliding Club. Ignore an early fork left, still above the trees, and continue rising until a pronounced right bend just past an old quarry. As the track eases, a small cairn sends a slender path straight on through the heather. Thin but clear, it runs on to terminate at a broad track: go right a few yards then turn left along another good track.

Back to our right are the hangars of the gliding club, a remarkable scar all round on a National Park moortop! **The track curves left and then right to merge into an initially wider track beneath boulders to the**

left. Go left along this track to descend gently to Brian's Pond.
During this the views include the long line of Cold Moor over to the
left, leading the eye into Raisdale, running into Bilsdale, and ahead to
Whorlton Moor overtopped by Black Hambleton.

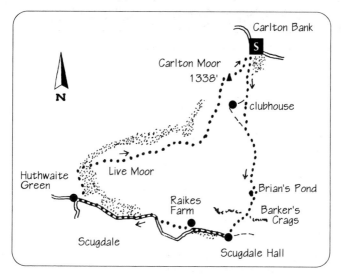

**Approaching a major fork just beyond the pond, opt for a less
obvious track branching right 15 yards short of the fork. This runs
along to a smaller, kidney shaped pool, with an adjacent mound of
uncertain origin. Beyond this the track suddenly dies on us. Keep
straight on through the heather a short way - bearing roughly south
- to pick up a thin trod. Go left on this to quickly emerge on a defined
edge overlooking Scugdale. The scattered rocks of Barker's Crags
should be in evidence beneath our edge, with the nearest buildings
being our objective of Scugdale Hall, below.** This is a real moment
to linger and absorb the supreme loveliness of Scugdale, deep and
green and thrusting into the heart of the moors.

**Paths run in from either side on this edge, while a sunken way slants
down to a bridle-gate behind the crumbling wall below.** Look back
up to appraise the great length of the scattered boulders of Barker's
Crags: some sections are substantial enough to attract rock climbers.
A path continues the slant down to the right end of a section of wall,

Carlton Moor from Live Moor

then drops down from the gate below to join a track by the farm. Turn right along the drive which becomes immediately surfaced. From Scugdale Hall a quiet, surfaced road leads unerringly down Scugdale to Huthwaite Green. This is a delightful section, regardless of it being on a hard surface: even devout non-road walkers will have little room to grumble.

At the first farm along the road (Raikes Farm) there is a chance to cut out a road section. Take a stile on the bend, immediately left of the buildings, and cross the paddock to gate and stile. Now slant down the large field to a stile part-way on (beyond a cluster of modern barns), and follow a couple of field-sides along to a tree-lined stream, a delightful bluebell dell. Up the other side a gap-stile returns us to the road to continue to Huthwaite Green.

Scugdale was mined for jet and ironstone, with a railway taking the latter out of the valley. Whilst walking down the lane note the extensive line of spoil heaps on the opposite hillside, indicating the consistent line of old workings. A track came down to the road junction at Huthwaite Green by the same route as we leave it. Huthwaite Green's entertainment value is limited to what can be done in a phone box. If in dire need of refreshment, Swainby is a mile and a half distant. At Huthwaite Green we pick up the route of the Cleveland Way and its followers, and work in recent years on the 'Cleveland Way Project' has seen much change in the nature of the path: expect lengthy sections to be on man-made stone ways.

At the T-junction leave the road by a fenced path rising to a wood. At the top note the grassy embankment of the old tramway scaling the slope in front. **Our way runs to the left before entering the trees at**

the far end. **A steep, well pitched climb leads quickly up through the trees onto the edge of the moor.** Immediately open views expand, featuring Roseberry Topping, and Carlton Moor itself projecting high ahead. A Faceby/Whorlton boundary stone is passed.

The path then rises ever gradually onto the crest of Live Moor. From Huthwaite Green to Carlton Moor the steep western scarp contrasts well with the heather carpet of the moor top to the right. This western scarp is littered with long abandoned jet and alum workings. The highest point of Live Moor is marked by a sprawling cairn, with views down into Scugdale. **A modest descent is made before a short pull onto the edge of Carlton Moor. The end of a glider runway is reached and this bizarre apparition shadows us along the edge. Only at the far end is it left behind to gain the Ordnance column and boundary stone at the moor's summit.**

Carlton Moor, like its eastern neighbours, rises gently from the south to a well defined top perched above a steep fall to the Cleveland Plain. This is a summit on which to linger - select a heathery couch beneath the exposed top and see how many communities can be identified with the aid of the OS map. The nearest, appropriately, is Carlton, literally at our feet. **The final descent is swift, the end already being in sight. The path keeps firmly above old alum workings to drop down to their right to soon regain the road at Carlton Bank.**

The summit of Carlton Moor, looking to Cringle Moor

CRINGLE MOOR

START   Carlton Bank   Grid ref. NZ 523030

DISTANCE   7 miles

ORDNANCE SURVEY MAPS
1:50,000
Landranger 93 - Middlesbrough & Darlington
1:25,000
Outdoor Leisure 26 North York Moors West

ACCESS Start on the summit of the Carlton-Chop Gate road above
Carlton Bank. There is a hidden car park just south of the brow.

A circuit of Cringle Moor using the flanks of its two neighbours, and
exploring far more than just Cringle. Not the gentlest walk in the book!

S   This walk neatly avoids climbs to all three nearby summits -
particularly if the jet miners' track is followed beneath Cringle End -
while still enjoying the glorious vistas and surroundings. For the
energetic any or all of them might be incorporated without a great deal
of trouble. Carlton and Cold Moors are visited in their own walks.

The summit of Carlton Bank has altered in recent years with the
provision of a cafe and car park. Though welcomed by us all, the cafe
is a particular boon to long distance walkers. It offers the only on-route
refreshment to Cleveland Wayfarers between Osmotherley and Kildale,
and to Coast to Coasters between Ingleby Arncliffe and the *Lion Inn*
on Blakey Ridge.

**Leave the car park by the rear, emerging onto a path that runs along
to the right to follow a fence to the foot of Cringle End. From a stile**
(that just yards to its left is a more level walk around the 'front' of the
hill, utilising the old jet miners' track) **a newly laid path climbs in the**

company of a wall to gain the prominent memorials on Cringle End.
Cringle End is one of those indefinable 'good places to be'. Perched
on its airy promontory are a memorial topograph and seat and also an
old boundary stone. **Here a mild surprise awaits, for the ground
continues rising further still, in dramatic fashion past the summit of
Cringle Moor.** Looking back Carlton Moor presents a fine shape, due
in part to the old quarries on it steep north face.

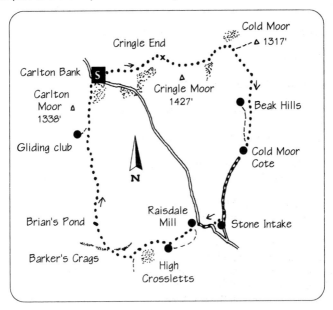

Cringle Moor is the second highest point on the North York Moors,
and is a good deal shapelier than Round Hill on Urra Moor. In step
with its loftier cousin its summit remains largely undisturbed by the
passing multitudes. The path directly above the dramatic plunge of its
steep north face boasts uninterrupted views of the plain and the other
hills. Flags dropped by helicopter add an unreal urban touch to the
scene.

**The steep descent path is also a recently creation, though this at least
is to be commended on what was a badly eroded and dangerous
section. Passing through a few spoil heaps head on to a wall corner.**

Just to the left a stubby old guidepost is inscribed 'Kirby Road North'. **From the gate at the end follow the wall round to rise towards the foot of Cold Moor.** Though the obvious way rises to a gate onto open fell then slants off the main path by rising right to a wall corner, there is a direct footpath available.

Part-way up the wall is a 4-way signpost. Turn right here ('Beak Hills') across the field to a gate, then slant up from the track to a gap-stile midway, continuing the slant up to another such stile in the intake wall. Joining a green track follow this along to the right for a good mile, passing above Beak Hills Farm and later joining its access road. This then passes by Cold Moor Cote and continues for a further mile to approach Stone Intake Farm. Just before it, take a stile on the right and descend a couple of fields to a gate onto the Raisdale road. Turn right to descend to cross a beck, and just up the other side turn down the drive to Raisdale Mill.

Cringle Moor, looking to Hasty Bank

Swing left between the buildings and immediately after the last on the right (the old mill) turn up a green hollowed way between trees. This is Raisdale Mill Lane, and is accompanied uphill until it emerges onto the moor. In wet conditions the farm road from Raisdale Mill to High Crossletts is a useful alternative.

Emerging at the head of the lane alongside High Crossletts, continue straight up a reedy corner onto the foot of the moor. A firm track soon crosses from the field on the left, and rises quickly towards the moor top. As it swings left above the wall, take a right fork (line of telegraph poles) to the brow of the hill. At a guidepost before

On Cringle End

Scugdale Gate leave the track and bear right across the heather to the end of the wall. Cross the stile there and head away on a super path, contouring round through a gap in the long line of Barker's Crags. Barker's Crags provide a perfect foreground to a prospect of the unfrequented green valley of Scugdale.

The path quickly bears round onto the heart of the moor, paralleling a sunken way to broaden out, soon reaching Brian's Pond. A long, gentle rise follows. As the track suddenly broadens substantially a junction is reached, with the hangars of the Newcastle & Teesside Gliding Club just ahead. Fork right to pass just below some prominent rocks up to the right.

After a large loop the track heads towards the gliding club. Just before emerging, a small cairn sends a slender trod* straight ahead through the heather: this quickly meets the end of a broad track. Cross straight over and resume in similar fashion (*If failing to locate this, go on to merge with another wide track: turn right along it a few yards, and at its immediate demise go left on the thin path). Ahead the Teesside prospect, including Roseberry Topping, returns to the scene. This slender path remains clear throughout and gradually descends to join the gliding club access track. This then descends more steeply to conclude the walk at Carlton Bank.

Cringle Moor from Cold Moor

SOME USEFUL ADDRESSES

Ramblers' Association 1/5 Wandsworth Road, London SW8 2XX
Tel. 0171-582 6878

North York Moors National Park Information Service
The Old Vicarage, Bondgate, Helmsley, York, YO6 5BP
Tel. 01439-770657

Information

Sutton Bank National Park Centre Tel. 01845-597426

14 Kirkgate **Thirsk** Tel. 01845-522755

Town Hall **Helmsley** Tel. 01439-770173

High Green **Great Ayton** Tel. 01642-722835

North Yorkshire Moors Association
7 The Avenue, Nunthorpe, Middlesbrough TS7 0AA
(not to be confused with the landowners' *Moorland Society*)

The National Trust Regional Office
Goddards, 27 Tadcaster Rd, York YO2 2QG Tel. 01904-702021

Friends of National Parks
Council for National Parks, Freepost, London SW11 1BR

Forestry Commission Forest Enterprise, 42 Eastgate, Pickering,
North Yorkshire YO18 7DU Tel. 01751-472771

Major bus operators

United Tel. 01325-468771

Tees & District Tel. 01642-210131

Moors Connections - *comprehensive transport timetables*
Elmtree Press & Distribution, The Elms, Exelby, Bedale, North Yorkshire DL8 2HD (send 50p for p + p)

LOG OF THE WALKS

WALK	DATE	NOTES
1		
2		
3		
4		
5		
6		
7		
8		
9		
10		
11		
12		
13		
14		
15		
16		
17		
18		
19		
20		
21		
22		
23		
24		
25		

INDEX

Principal features: walk number refers